RESTORING OLD HOUSES

*One of
the conditions of
aesthetic taste seems to be
that in civilised life
it shall revolve in cycles.*

CHARLES L EASTLAKE
Hints on Household Taste
1868

Elevation of proposed villas, Malvern,
Victoria, by C D Figgis, architect, Victoria
Buildings, Melbourne, c. 1890

RESTORING OLD HOUSES

Ian Evans

M

First published 1979 by
THE MACMILLAN COMPANY OF AUSTRALIA PTY LTD
107 Moray Street, South Melbourne 3205
6 George Place, Artarmon 2064
Reprinted 1980

Associated companies in
London and Basingstoke, England
New York Dublin Johannesburg Delhi

National Library of Australia
cataloguing in publication data

Evans, Ian.
    Restoring old houses.

    Index
    Bibliography
    ISBN 0 333 29881 0

    1. Architecture, Domestic — Australia — Conservation
    and Restoration. I. Title.

728.64'0994

Set in Bembo by Savage & Co., Brisbane
Printed in Hong Kong

Foreword

By Clive Lucas, O B E, B. Arch., F R A I A

Australia has a rich heritage of Victorian and Edwardian houses in country towns and in what have become the inner suburbs of the coastal cities. After long periods of neglect these houses are now being appreciated. Each year thousands are upgraded as places for twentieth-century families to live. In almost every case this rehabilitation includes what is loosely termed 'restoration'. The tragedy is that in most cases it is not restoration at all. The term is widely misunderstood and wrongly applied.

Often these houses are part of significant groups of similar buildings. Their exteriors are important, not just because of their individual merits, but because of their relationship to their neighbours and to their environment. External details contribute to the overall effect. Bootscrapers, shutters, knockers, panelled doors, garden edging tiles, fencing, stuccoed decoration, planting and colours all enrich a district's character. Inside, there are many features of particular interest. The lock on the front door, the tiles and the grate in the fireplace, the plaster ceiling roses and cornices, finger plates, door furniture, original colour schemes and other forms of decoration. It is usually this sort of detail that disappears when a building is being rehabilitated, often simply because it is not recognised as original.

A common error is the removal of external render, or stucco as it was known, to reveal the brickwork. Almost all nineteenth-century housing was stuccoed to imitate stone. This was not just an aesthetic conceit but a technical necessity; the porous bricks were covered to prevent the absorption of moisture. Removal of the render alters the historic character of the house and increases the risk of moisture problems. In the kitchen, pantry and other back rooms, interior walls of brick or stone were often implastered but were always painted, and this should be appreciated. Another error is to strip paint from joinery which in fact may always have been painted. Original decorative treatments are thus lost.

This book attempts to correct the many misunderstandings concerning our Victorian and Edwardian housing stock. In an illuminating and interesting text, Ian Evans not only gives us the background from many original sources but also the approach to solving the problems demanded by authentic restoration.

Restoring Old Houses will be welcomed by all those who are interested in preserving the character of Victorian or Edwardian houses but who until now have had nowhere to turn for assistance.

Acknowledgements

A great many people helped to make this book possible. Many of them were strangers who shared the author's concern for old houses. I thank them all and hope they will feel that the results have justified their efforts.

A small group must be singled out for particular thanks. It includes Patrick Crowe, Annette Evans, Brendan Kelly, Clive Lucas, Pat McArdell, Denis and Raina Robinson, and Alan Townsend.

My thanks to the following are equally sincere: Richard Allom, Brian Baldwin, Judy Birmingham, James Broadbent, Bruce Buchanan, Keith Burley, Robin Campbell, Darien Cassidy, Barry Cooper, Robert Cutts, Mari Davis, Denise Fawcett, Warwick Forge, Stewart Game, Robert Halliday, Shirley Hawker, Shar Jones, Theo Lamb, Jenny Lane, Rita Liseo, Kevin Little, Robert Longhurst, Bill and Fred Mashman, Peter Mercer, Athol Munday, Bren O'Dowd, Timo Savimaki, Don and Jan Tomsett, John Wade; and many others, including the staff of the National Trust offices in various States; the staff of the Battye Library, Perth; the South Australian State Library; the John Oxley Library, Brisbane; the Latrobe Library, Melbourne; the Mitchell Library, Sydney; the State Library of Tasmania; and the Tasmanian Museum and Art Gallery.

Contents

Introduction

The period from 1837 to 1910, from the accession of Queen Victoria to the death of Edward VII, spans seventy-three years in which great changes occurred not only in architecture but in every other aspect of life in Australia. It was not until around the middle of the nineteenth century that the colonial phase of our national architecture, with its Georgian, Regency and vernacular influences, ended and a truly Victorian style began to evolve. The broad stream of Victorian architecture actually accommodated a variety of sub-styles, each with its own particular attributes.

The decade from 1890 to 1900 saw an overlapping of styles. The last years of Victorian architecture were shared with the radically different Federation style with its emphasis on a return to honesty in the use of natural materials in building construction. Its characteristics included the use of red brick, high roofs of red Marseilles tiles or slate, ornamental ridge cappings, towers, turrets, wide verandahs, and the use of leadlight or coloured glass panels to windows and doors. The woodwork to gables, porches and verandahs was invariably painted white. Art nouveau exerted a powerful influence on this style which achieved its greatest popularity during the Edwardian period. Houses in the Federation style were still being built as late as 1920 although the style as an architectural movement can be considered to have come to an end by the beginning of World War I.

RESTORATION, NOT RENOVATION

The purpose of this volume is to set out broad guidelines and provide a basis upon which to approach the restoration of Victorian and Edwardian houses. The essential ingredient in any restoration project is familiarity with the style of the building. This can best be achieved by careful study of comparable buildings of the same style and period. It is

Cottages near Thornleigh, N S W, designed by Cyril Blacket, architect, 1903, and built by William Knowles for £1186

hoped that the information provided here will complement a study of actual Victorian and Edwardian houses and at the same time generate a new interest in this period of Australian architecture.

From the subdivision plan of the Campsie Park Estate, N S W, 1885

After generations of neglect, indifference and dislike there is now a revived awareness of the character and unique appeal of the houses of Victorian and Edwardian Australia. The politicians and planners who for years worked on ambitious schemes to bulldoze slums, so called, and replace them with blocks of flats have quietly faded away. No-one speaks anymore of the 'grey ring of blight' which was said to surround Sydney and, by inference, other major Australian cities.

Community attitudes began to change in the 1960s and 1970s as increasing numbers of young people moved into the inner city to minimise travel to and from work. They brought with them a new awareness of the environment and an appreciation of the history and architecture of the older suburbs in which they settled. So began the movement which has led to the regeneration of thousands of houses in the inner suburbs and has rescued many valuable buildings from continued deterioration and probable demolition.

INNER-SUBURBAN DECAY

Two major factors contributed to the degradation of the older areas of our larger cities: the flight of the original middle-class residents, and the inability of succeeding generations of working-class tenants and homeowners to ensure that ageing properties received the maintenance that they required.

Deterioration began this century, but its origins are complex and lie much further

Front Elevation

back. The development of improved transport systems towards the end of the nineteenth century enabled more desirable developments to be opened up further from the heart of the cities and enticed more prosperous homeowners to move to the new suburbs. Their homes, which had been made less manageable as domestic staff became more difficult to obtain, were sold and frequently divided into flats and rooms by their new proprietors. In the process of conversion, partition walls closed off the larger rooms, while kitchens and bathrooms were provided in what had once been dining rooms, drawing rooms, bedrooms or balconies. The original decor, by now no longer fashionable, was painted or otherwise obliterated.

The middle-class exodus may have been hastened by the contempt with which some influential members of the architectural profession regarded popular housing fashions of the late nineteenth century. They spoke of 'shocking cast iron designs', of 'atrocious ornaments' and of suburban streets . . .

> hedged with interminable rows of ochre-tinted terraces, with their hideous iron balconies and preposterous parapets—those plastered and whited sepulchres, in which if existence is practicable it is at least impossible to live? Nothing can redeem them from their squalid ugliness; no amount of colour could ever impart to them one touch of beauty.[1]

That attack, by the architect J B Barlow in 1892, was typical of many made at the time on lower middle-class and working-class housing, particularly as the new Federation style became fashionable. Although most of the criticism was aired in professional circles and in industry journals the attitudes expressed eventually began to filter through the community. It was not long before the middle class began to leave the inner urban areas.

The process of deterioration continued throughout most of this century and did not begin to be arrested on a large scale until well into the 1970s. The work of the various state National Trusts and, more recently, of the Australian Heritage Commission in recognising and protecting the nation's legacy of Victorian and Edwardian architecture has contributed greatly to the recent change in public attitudes.

Most of the work that must be done is in the hands of the people, often quite young and inexperienced, who plunge their savings into the purchase of dilapidated houses in suburbs that have seen better days. The way they carry out their tasks is of considerable importance, not only to those who treasure the concept of the National Estate, but to the owners themselves. Renovations carried out in accordance with some fashionable whim detract from the aesthetic and architectural significance of an old house and, in a comparatively short space of time, will diminish rather than enhance the value of the building. Houses restored in sympathy with the intentions of the original designer and builder can be expected to command premium prices on the real estate market. There is thus a very real financial incentive for the authentic restoration of old houses.

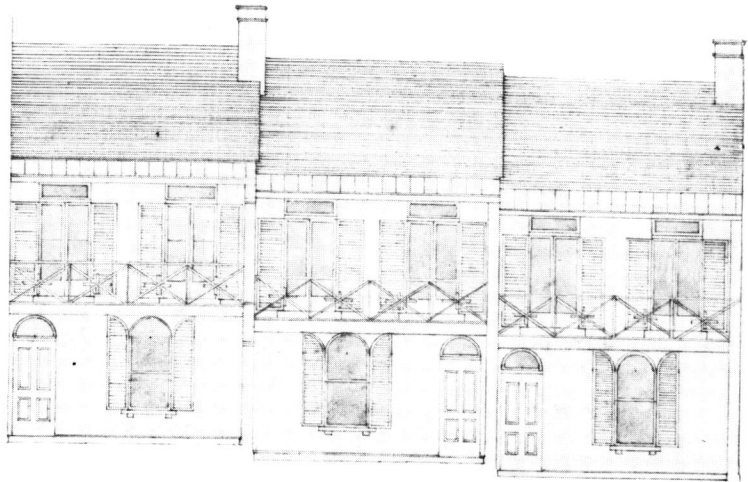

Houses for Mr Grant, by Edmund Blacket, architect, c. 1870s

UNSYMPATHETIC ALTERATION

It is to be regretted that so much money and effort is poured into totally unsympathetic alterations to the diminishing numbers of Victorian and Edwardian houses. Many worthwhile buildings are being ruined in a process which attracts none of the public attention that is concentrated when one particularly important building is about to be demolished. It could be argued that the process of gradual destruction, most marked in the inner suburbs of the major cities, constitutes a greater damage to the fabric of the National Estate than does the demolition of the occasional grand house or public building.

Most of the damage is done in the name of property 'improvement'. Aluminium windows replace the original double-hung sash windows; fireplaces and chimneys are removed; the stucco or render is stripped from facades to expose sandstock bricks; and forbidding walls are erected to hide the house from the street. Each such act constitutes a small tragedy.

Action to halt this carnage is urgently required. External alterations to houses in historic areas, or individual houses more than seventy years old and which are considered by an acknowledged authority to be worthy of preservation, should be firmly discouraged, if not forbidden. Protection of such buildings will probably require a concerted effort by both state and local government and may involve the imposition of protective zonings and appropriate legislation. Perhaps, as an election approaches, an alert political party may promise to introduce a comprehensive system of grants for the improvement of old houses, similar to those provided in France, the Netherlands, the United States and Great Britain. It is not sufficient to ban demolition or unsympathetic alteration; authentic restoration requires funds and expertise.

Restoration may be defined as the process by which a building is taken back to the form and appearance which it held at a particular period in time. It is more time-consuming and expensive than new construction and requires considerable energy and commitment. It is not a task to be lightly undertaken.

Once the commitment has been made, however, restoration can become an intellectual exercise offering a glimpse into the lifestyle of past generations and into the near-forgotten techniques of the craftsmen of the nineteenth century. The dedicated restorer will acquire some of the expertise of a variety of trades and techniques, including several which are virtually unknown today, combined with the research skills of a social historian. The appreciation and understanding of architecture and building, in the various phases which were in vogue between 1840 and 1910, will be greatly enhanced.

During the process of restoring an old house information will be accumulated on its builders, early owners and occupants, and their place in the society of the time. It should be possible to determine when a house was built and to gain an inkling of the source of some of the materials used in its construction. The name of the first owner should be obtainable fairly readily. In some cases it will be possible to discover not only the name of the builder and architect, but the cost of construction.

The transition in architectural styles that took place in the 1890s is illustrated by these houses in the Sydney suburb of Glebe. The houses in the foreground are decorated with cast-iron while their neighbour, built at the same time, features turned timber for the columns of its balcony. Timber was one of the principal decorative elements in the Australian Edwardian style known as Federation

AN AIR OF FADED ELEGANCE

Architects engaged on restoration projects overseas, where buildings many centuries old may be involved, have to face complex problems of a type which seldom arise in the context of this book. We do not have to try to date ancient buildings nor decide how to approach the restoration of a house that may have been constructed in one century and added to by various owners during succeeding centuries. The question 'To what period or style do you restore?' is usually comparatively simply answered in our case.

In most cases additions and alterations will be quite unsympathetic. However, changes which are considered to be in harmony with the approach of the original architect or builder may be retained. Probably the most appropriate approach to be taken to the restoration of an old house is to seek to give it the feeling of a building which has been cared for during a long and satisfying life. It will be well painted and decorated and have the appearance of having been properly maintained. But there will perhaps be an air of gentle decadence—the patina of time. This approach allows for some imperfections, particularly with minor elements of Victoriana or Edwardiana which cannot easily be repaired or replaced.

The restoration of badly abused Victorian or Edwardian houses can be assisted by a careful study of contemporary buildings. Other houses in a group offer the very best comparison for those who are trying to piece together information that will ensure the authenticity of their own restoration project. Although there will be varying degrees of difference between the houses in a group of terraces, the overall pattern and style will be the same. Most builders ordered fittings in bulk to finish off every house in a terraced group. Locks, fingerplates, cast iron, chimneypieces, fences and brassware should be identical in every house constructed as part of a group. What is missing from one house may often be seen in another.

DEMOLITION: AN UNPLEASANT FACT

Throughout this book reference is made to acquiring various items from demolition sites or demolition contractors. This is not to be construed as implying approval of the wholesale demolition of old houses: it is no more than a recognition of the fact that such demolition occurs. At present there is usually no other way to obtain the hardware, fixtures and other items which are essential to the restoration of cherished houses.

It could be argued that a very large proportion of the old houses demolished in Australia today were not at the end of their economic life. They are often demolished simply because developers lack either the imagination or the initiative to restore them. It is easier

A turret and elaborate timber columns are important features of this imposing Federation-style house in Chandos Street, Ashfield, N S W. Its original roof of slate or Marseilles tiles has been replaced

to clear the site and start again. Where local government planning schemes permit, an old house in poor condition on a large site is almost certain to be razed to make way for home units. The financial return from such a venture ensures that the old building does not survive. Victorian or Edwardian houses are frequently swallowed up in the expansion of shopping centres. A few may survive, transformed into restaurants or professional offices but usually tarted up in the extreme.

Where old houses must be demolished the job should be done properly, with care taken to ensure that significant items are available for re-use. Too often an impatient demolition contractor will ruin valuable items which he could have sold at a considerable profit. Panelled doors, perhaps of cedar, are wrenched from their hinges with pinch-bars. Other items, often equally valuable, go to the tip.

This is needless waste. A well-advertised demolition will usually result in the sale and re-use of all of the important component parts of a doomed building. Visiting a demolition site can be a moving experience for a lover of old houses, torn between jubilation at acquiring some long-sought item and regret at the often unnecessary loss of yet another part of the National Estate.

LIMITS OF AUTHENTICITY

It should be made clear at this point that there is no recommendation in this book for the complete restoration of houses of the nineteenth or early twentieth century. Such restoration would require the creation of museums with every room, including kitchens, bathrooms and bedrooms, finished and furnished as they were when first occupied. There would be no labour-saving appliances, no television sets or radios and, in the majority of cases, no telephones.

Compromise is the only realistic approach. An acceptable formula is to settle for the restoration of the exterior of the house, its front fence and garden, and, in the interior, the authentic treatment of the entrance hall, drawing room and dining room. Ideally, the furniture and furnishings in these rooms should be contemporary with the date of the house but this is a matter that can only be decided by the taste and financial means of the individual owner. Kitchens and bathrooms may be modernised while bedrooms and other private areas may be decorated and furnished as required.

In adopting this approach allowances should be made for the special features that individual houses may have retained. The kitchen, for example, may still be fitted with an old cast-iron cooking range which, if space permits, should be kept.

Australians in their homes

A brief history, 1840–1910

Design for a cottage for Mr Anivette, by William Boles, architect, Sydney, 1876

Pembroke Terrace, Buckingham Street, Sydney, January 1871. Note the uniformity of design and finish

The dominant housing form in Victorian and Edwardian Australia was the terrace. An attached row of houses of a uniform style, it was constructed to a simple basic plan that was capable of seemingly infinite variation. It provided acceptable shelter to the families of humble working men or assuaged the higher aspirations of the middle classes. There was always a wealthy minority, of course, which felt comfortable only in free-standing cottages or villas.

HOUSING FASHIONS

The terrace had originated in London where the techniques of building and estate development on the outskirts of a major city had been evolved and refined since the seventeenth century. It was soon realised that terraced housing had much to recommend it from the point of view of both the building speculator and the homeowner. Because it reduced the area of land that each house required, it lowered the total cost of housing and offered the advantages of home ownership to a wider cross-section of the population, providing houses to many not able to afford the luxury of a free-standing cottage or villa.

While terrace houses occupied only a comparatively small site, they gave their occupants an abundance of living space. There were other advantages. Terraces perfectly suited the scale of cities and large towns in an age when transport systems were primitive and beyond the means of the majority of the people. A suburb of terraces was compact and easily traversed on foot.

The terrace was economical of materials. Common dividing or 'party' walls offered

From the subdivision plan of the Campsie Park Estate, N S W, 1885

savings in bricks, mortar and labour that amounted to a substantial sum in a row of terraces, let alone an entire suburb. Other economies were made on the roof, fencing, plumbing and drainage, and exterior painting. Terraces were usually two-storied and could be constructed in groups of from two to twelve or more houses, depending on the land that was available and the resources of the developer. Other reasons for their popularity arose from limitations of building technology which were not overcome until the late nineteenth century. A two-storied house had less contact with the ground, thus minimising the possible effects of rising damp.

But the most significant reason for the proliferation of the terrace was the fact that it offered the speculator maximum return on his investment.

INFLUENCES ON AUSTRALIAN ARCHITECTURE

There were many changes in Australian architecture between 1840 and 1910. It is not intended to explore them in detail here, for volumes could be written about each of them: the late colonial era with its post-Regency cottages, and later in the nineteenth century the styles known as picturesque Gothic, Italianate, and Federation. The major influences cast upon nineteenth-century Australia, in architecture, furniture, dress, manners or speech, were of course British. To all but a few nationalists, whatever was done in London was the model of perfection. British books on architecture and every aspect of the construction and decoration of houses were on the shelves of public and private libraries throughout the Australian colonies within a year or two of their publication.

However, the thoughts of the leading British critic of Victoriana, Charles L Eastlake, do not appear to have been as well received in Australia as they were in Britain and the United States. Eastlake despised the Victorian taste for ornament and the practice of treating one material in such a way that it appeared to be another. He found many easy targets in domestic architecture where cheap timber was grained to resemble mahogany or walnut and wallpaper simulating marble was hung in entrance halls. To Eastlake, the cast-iron ornamentation that began to appear on many houses from the 1840s onward was 'a mean and spiritless system of decoration'.

The practice of rendering or stuccoing the outside walls of buildings and marking the surface with grooves to imitate the appearance of stone drew from him a bitter blast: 'In an evil hour stucco was invented . . . ., Australian architects and builders were still employing most of the devices he detested until the early twentieth century.

GROWING NATIONALISM

Although the British tradition in architecture and design was to linger in Australia for many years the upsurge in national spirit that occurred throughout the Australian colonies was reflected in many of the houses built during the 1890s, despite the effects on the building industry of a severe economic slump. Journals such as the *Australasian Builder and Contractors' News* urged architects and builders to express the increasing sense of nationalism.

Restored terraces, Woolloomooloo, N S W. The modern light fittings are a lapse in detailing

Carleith, *Gladstone Avenue, Hunter's Hill, N S W*

... we have hitherto been getting our architecture at second-hand from England, and hence it is as conventional as the cut of our coats. Why can we not free ourselves from the fetters of this conventionality, and erect buildings more suited to our requirements ... quite irrespective of English precedent?[2]

In the atmosphere of fervid patriotism generated by the possibility of Federation, native wildflowers and birds began to appear in the decoration of houses that in most other respects were British. Terraces that could have been quietly slipped into the streets of London began to display Australian motifs in their cast iron decoration, in the etched and coloured glass at their front doors, and on the ceramic tiles that adorned their facades and hearths.

This movement was promoted by the artist Lucien Henry, an instructor at the Sydney Technical College, who in the 1880s prepared a pattern book for architects and craftsmen:

M. Henry has conceived and elaborated the happy idea of founding a distinctively Australian order of architecture ... by the application to it of designs and colours borrowed from our indigenous fauna and flora, selecting for treatment ... the lyre bird and the Tasmanian hippocampus, and the waratah, the stenocarpus, the protea, the actinotus, the stag's horn fern, the mangrove, the screw-palm, and the gigantic lily of Queensland.[3]

Henry's book was never published, but his ideas were adopted by other architects and translated into forms which were acceptable in the marketplace. His designs had included a waratah electrolier and a cornice featuring an aboriginal's head.[4]

As the turn of the century approached the new Federation style, with its emphasis on natural materials, began to make its mark. The facades of houses throughout the colonies were increasingly decorated with turned and fretted wood. The Victorian fashion for cast iron had begun to fade.

Beryl Lee, *a late Edwardian cottage in Ross Street, Glebe, N S W, is an excellent example of* Federation-*style architecture*

A terrace of shingle-roofed cottages in Pulteney Street, Adelaide, photographed c. 1890

This sketch of Montana, *a Federation-style villa, is by its architects, A L and G McCredie, and was published in the* Australasian Builder and Contractor's News *on 26 November 1892 (see bottom of page)*

ARCHITECTS, BUILDERS, HOMEOWNERS, TENANTS AND LANDLORDS

The men responsible for building the homes of Victorian and Edwardian Australians were a highly diverse group with a great range of skills. Many had entered the building industry through apprenticeship to a bricklayer, stonemason, carpenter, plasterer, or one of the lesser-known trades. It was common for such men, after some years in their trade, to become speculative builders. They picked up designs from pattern books, from architects, or prepared their own. Houses built by these men usually lacked the polish of buildings which had been designed by a professionally-trained architect and constructed under his supervision. There are rows of terraces, still standing today, which were designed and built by men without formal qualifications of any kind.

Innovation was not their game. They were safe so long as they kept to familiar ground—stucco, cast iron, and all the comfortable architectural mannerisms of the age. This conservatism infuriated the avant garde who launched vitriolic attacks on what they saw as the depressing familiarity of contemporary Australian housing: '. . . we are brought face to face with a general, an almost universal, a dreary, dirty, dusty, drab-hued dinginess of desert-like depression, which seems to fill the very soul with sadness, and predisposes almost to suicide.'[5]

GENTLEMEN WHO INTEND BUILDING

ARE INVITED BY

MR. HAROLD BREES,

ARCHITECT,

MORT'S PASSAGE, GEORGE STREET, SYDNEY,

TO INSPECT HIS

ELEGANT DESIGNS OF VILLA RESIDENCES,

CONSISTING OF ABOVE 100 DESIGNS AND PLANS,

in every style of

RURAL ARCHITECTURE.

The Designs having been drawn to suit the CLIMATE OF AUSTRALIA.

And in the Plans the greatest consideration having been employed with regard to COMFORT, ECONOMY, and VENTILATION.

Highest References, and Moderate Charges.

PERRY'S HOTEL,

From Sands' Sydney Directory *for 1866*

JERRY-BUILDERS, THEN AS NOW
Critics saved their worst invective for the jerry-builders, speculators and unscrupulous architects who profited at public expense.

> . . . must the general public continue to reside in dwellings built by the 'jerry' architect and 'jerry' builder, or 'run up' by that arch-fiend, the Australasian speculative landlord . . .?[6]

Montana, *in Boyce Street, Glebe, N S W. The house was built for Alfred Whetton junior in 1892*

House for Mrs Andreas by the Sydney architects, Blacket Brothers, c. 1880

The ground floor plan of the house for Mrs Andreas

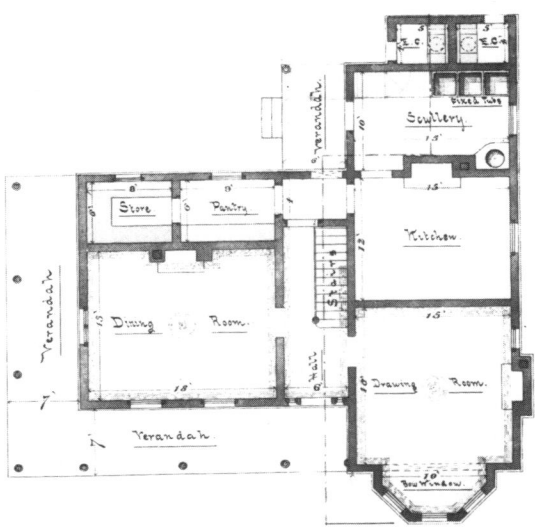

In many cases the jerry landlord or land-owner is the true *raison de etre* [sic] of the jerry builder. The landlord is frequently . . . a man who has 'worked his way up' and 'wants to build a few houses as an investment.' His main object is to get as high a return for his money as he can, and to do this he crowds . . . as many dwellings as he can upon a certain piece of ground. He knows that small dwellings letting at a weekly rent to artizans and other people drawing their wages every Saturday are the least risky tenement-property as regards returns . . . . He himself is entirely ignorant of the rudiments of sanitary science . . . and anxious only to get the dwellings 'run up' and 'occupied.'

He goes, perhaps, to a jerry architect . . . who 'makes a set' of jerry 'plans' and a jerry builder 'puts in a price' for the 'job.' The 'builder' . . . having taken the 'job' at a starvation price for the 'advantage' of securing the work of such an invaluable 'patron,' and who naturally wants to make a few pounds out of it for himself, proceeds to do so by scamping those parts of the work that he thinks his 'patron' is not likely to bother himself about examining before they are covered up. Floors are laid upon the damp earth; green and 'shuffy' bricks are used in walls which spring up as if by magic; 'drains' of the kind used in the Garden of Eden are 'laid down'—and the germs of deadly maladies along with them . . . .[7]

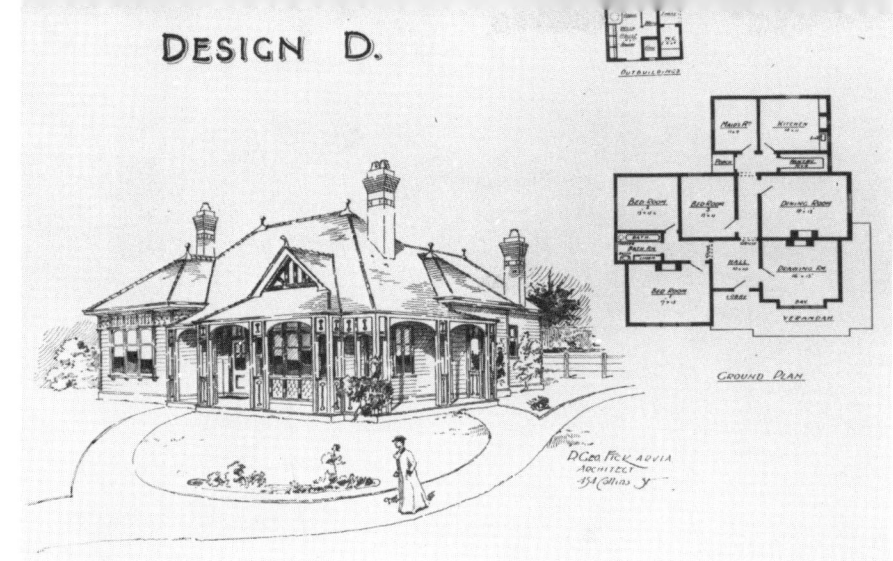

DESIGN D.

An Edwardian villa in the Federation-style by the Melbourne architect R George Fick. From a catalogue used by a builder on the Moreland Grove subdivision

At a time when it was possible for anyone to screw a brass plate to his door, an architect could be someone with the highest qualifications in the aesthetics of art and design, draughtmanship, estimating and the framing of specifications, or a former carpenter or bricklayer who saw the profession as a short cut to status and wealth: 'We know instances in which auctioneers and house-agents, who can scarcely tell the difference between a set-square and a protractor, have suddenly bloomed into full-fledged "architects" without having any previous training whatever.'[8]

The role of the unqualified and less confident 'architects' was simplified by the use of pattern books. These provided a range of plans and sketches for houses large and small, and in many different designs. A client might be permitted to browse through the books until he found something that suited. An alternative practice was for the architect to resort to his pattern books in the privacy of his office and to reproduce in his own hand, perhaps with variations, the plans which he believed would be of interest to his client. Where original designs were attempted there were methods to ensure their success.

> . . . you cannot do better than adopt Professor Kerr's ingenious device for shaking your ground-plan into shape. This consists simply in cutting out pieces of cardboard corresponding to the sizes of the required rooms, so that one card may represent the dining-room, another the library, another the breakfast parlour, and so on; and then bringing the separate pieces together, so as to group the whole into a convenient plan.'[9]

A WOMAN'S PLACE

Women were seldom consulted, or even considered, when houses were being planned in the nineteenth century. Housewives and maids alike had to make do with what men considered to be practical, efficient layouts for their kitchen, pantry, scullery and laundry. The authors of *Working Drawings and Designs in Architecture and Building* cautiously put forward a radical idea when their book was published in 1866—the advice of women should be sought before construction began.

> It might seem, at first sight, beneath the dignity of an architect to take counsel—while engaged in planning a house—from a housewife. . . . There are few houses built . . . the arrangements and conveniences of which could not be modified with advantage after taking a housewife—who knows what work there is in a house to do, and how to do it—through all its apartments, and asking her opinion about them; how far they are calculated to promote or hinder economy and convenience. . . . Doubtless it will be objected that there will be difficulty in getting such a counsellor to understand the intricacies of a plan. But this . . . understanding of a plan by the female mind, is not after all so difficult a matter as is, or might be, supposed.[10]

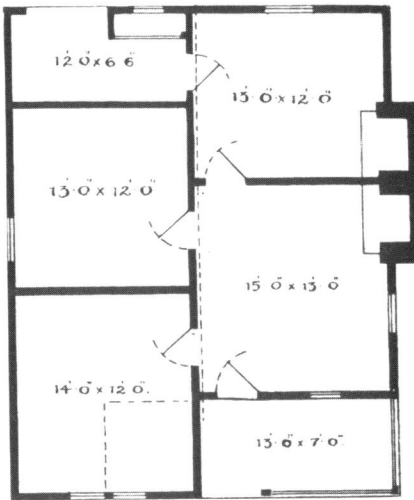

Sketch and floor plan of a simple Edwardian cottage. From the Kauri Timber Company's 50 Modern Ideal Cottage Homes, *1901*

19

The humble cottages of working men, restored to their 1870s appearance, in Mitchell Street, Glebe, N S W. The striped verandah roofs and picket fences are original features which have been replaced

It is doubtful whether many colonial 'female minds' were taxed with the intricacies of housing plans as the builders and developers set about the task of covering the cow paddocks and native bush on the fringes of Australian cities with speculative cottages and terraces.

CLASS AND HOUSING

Social divisions were far more clearly marked in the nineteenth century than they are today. A vast gulf separated the comfortable middle classes from those in the working classes. Middle-class family-men owned their houses and took a carriage, the omnibus or a hackney cab to their office; artisans rented their homes and walked to work. It was not until late in the nineteenth century that developments in transport technology, lower fares and higher wages brought the regular use of public transport within reach of the ordinary workman or lower-grade clerk.

Such divisions were very clearly stated in the architecture of the era and are easily discernable in the size, quality, materials and ornamentation of existing Victorian and Edwardian housing. With few exceptions, the homes of the very poor have not survived. These were mostly mean shacks of timber or brick, thrown together by enterprising capitalists anxious to take advantage of the great increase in population that occurred throughout the colonies in the last three decades of the nineteenth century. The pressure on housing resources caused concern for the plight of the working classes but it was much easier to define the problem than to take effective action to counter it. Dr James Neild probably shocked his audience at a Melbourne lecture in 1872 when he said: 'Nothing that I ever witnessed in the West Riding of Yorkshire and in South Lancashire, equalled in repulsiveness what I have found in Melbourne. There are hundreds of dwellings, but a few yards out of our busiest thoroughfares ... [that are] literally heaps of rotting filth.'[11]

A statement nineteen years later by the architect G C Inskip, also of Melbourne, indicates that very little improvement had occurred: 'The working classes ... are compelled, in many instances, to dwell in the shoddy houses erected by greedy speculators, without proper drainage or ventilation. The rent of these death-traps being also excessive ....'[12]

There was, in most cases, very little wrong with the houses themselves. The faults lay in the sewerage, drainage, and water-supply systems. Open cesspits, shared water closets and contaminated wells were commonplace. Death from typhoid fever and other serious illnesses was a common occurrence. In 1900 bubonic plague struck in Adelaide and Sydney where it took 103 lives, chiefly residents of the poorer districts of the city.[13]

Edwardian houses from the Moreland Grove subdivision, Victoria

The problem posed by unhealthy sewerage systems in the Sydney suburb of Parramatta compelled an anonymous author to offer the following contribution to the *Australasian Builder and Contractors' News* where it was published on October 10, 1891:

THE SONG OF THE SEWAGE
A Parramatta Plaint

(Parramatta, N S W,
like Hamlet, 'has that within which
passes outward show')

*   *   *

Squatter and pauper, M.P. and waif,
From unseen atoms are not safe:
Beauty and virtue, vice and glare,
Are levelled by Parramatta air.

*   *   *

Pure air, food, water, dainties to lure,
Tainted by filth—disease from the sewer—
A fatal source, beyond control,
Of mighty atoms that kill the soul.

*   *   *

To breath God's air, without fear or dismay,
Parramatta 'petitioners ever pray.'
Sewage-Poisoned Parramatta

This simple timber cottage at Burnie in north-west Tasmania was typical of housing provided for workers employed by the Van Diemen's Land Company. The photograph dates from about 1900

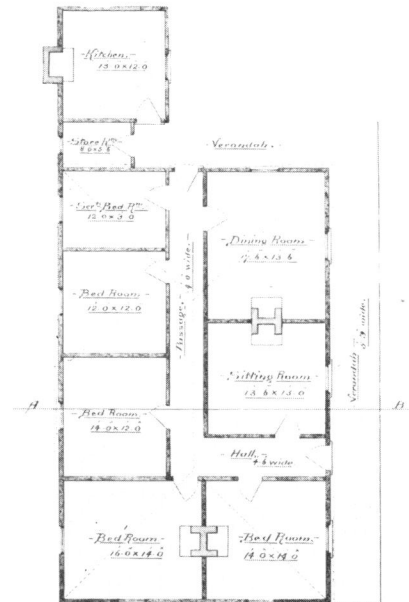

Plan of a cottage at Avoca, N S W, for Mr Clements, by Arthur Blacket of Sydney

*A comment on nineteenth-century sanitary
and water supply systems. From the*
Australasian Builder and Contractors'
News, *10 October 1891*

The population of metropolitan Sydney increased from 138 000 in 1871 to 496 000 in 1901. Comparable increases were recorded in the other capitals. On the outskirts of the major cities orchards and cow-paddocks were quickly laid out into streets and covered with rows of neat cottages which, until the depression of the 1890s, were sold and occupied almost as swiftly as they were constructed. James Inglis, in his book *Our Australian Cousins*, depicted suburban development in the 1870s as spreading 'like a lava flood'.[14]

Suburban extension is proceeding with wonderful speed. Everywhere the sound of the workmen's tools is heard, all through the busy day. Brick-yards are worked to their greatest powers, saw-mills and joinery establishments are in full activity and at present the building trades are in constant and vigorous employment.

Inglis felt that the results of all this feverish activity reflected great credit on those who had been largely responsible for initiating it.

Even the less pretentious structures bear many marks of good taste, and an advanced order of embellishment. Indeed, the suburban villas of Sydney inhabited by the well-to-do tradesmen, the highly intelligent, quick-witted, practical, money-making middle classes, give one a high opinion of the material prosperity, and the solid domestic comfort which their appearance implies.

With no real supervision of their activities, it is astonishing that so few builders engaged in the practices condemned by the trade journals: 'The lowest-priced bricks, and the sloppiest of workmanship, plenty of plaster and paint, and then the production is sold to some good easy man who thinks he has acquired an honest dwelling at a bargain.'[15]

It was not only the working class who were exploited. Middle class wealth, recently accumulated in boom conditions, offered excellent prospects for the less scrupulous developers. The eminent architect Howard Joseland did not approve of the results:

. . . the bounds of Art in building were overstepped in the craze to produce new wonders that would appeal to the tastes of those who had suddenly risen from humble life by an unexpected share of commercial plunder. . . . As an outcome of all this, we see hideous sketches of terraces and wildernesses of villas in painted brick or cement, decked with meaningless ironwork and atrocious ornaments.'[16]

It might fairly be said that this was an elitist attitude and reflected more of the speaker's prejudices and the divisions that were then evident within the profession of architecture than the reality of the situation. The professionals who prided themselves on being a cut above their self-made colleagues spent a great deal of time pondering and discussing the qualities of the Greek temples. The problem of providing housing for a soaring population was not worth discussing. They descended from their Olympian clouds only to criticise and attack.

Architects and other commentators virtually ignored the achievements of the vast majority of builders and tradesmen, the evidence of whose skilled and honest work can still be seen in cities and towns throughout Australia. Today, as many of these houses enter their second century, there is new appreciation of their aesthetic and historic significance, and of their value as a unique testimony to the skills of Victorian and Edwardian architects, builders and tradesmen.

A family gathering in the Pittsworth district of Queensland, c. 1899

Top: Hobart, c. 1900; middle: Richmond, Tasmania, c. 1890; below: a house in South Australia, c. 1900

THE PEOPLE AT HOME

On reaching Argyle Street, I turned up it as far as Cambridge Street . . . . This was not lighted by gas and [was] by no means a smooth footway for a pitch dark night. Cold damp unwholesome smells assailed the nose . . . . But strange to say perfect quiet reigned here; every cottage was closed up and the blinds were drawn. In the lighter parts of the Rocks, Gloucester and Cumberland Streets, there [were] . . . a few people gossiping at the corners, or moving homewards. Princes Street was perfectly quiet except for the subdued murmur of conversation inside the dwellings . . . [which] was in almost every part of the town audible. The interior of all the dwellings too, with few exceptions, appeared cheerful where a glimpse could be obtained. The family was generally round the central table or sitting about on chairs and sofa. The females were generally engaged in needlework; all were talking.[17]

Greater understanding of the architecture of the nineteenth century comes with insight into the pattern of the lives of the people of the age; their working conditions, transport and family life. The account of William Stanley Jevons, quoted above, of an evening stroll through one of the poorer areas of Sydney, the Rocks, on November 10, 1858, conveys all the atmosphere of life in an Australian city in the mid-nineteenth century as well as providing an illuminating account of the way of life of ordinary people, relaxing at home after the day's work was done.

Technological development and the vast social changes that have occurred since the turn of the century have served to obscure our understanding of the way of life of earlier generations of Australians. Some of the factors involved in this slow but far-reaching process of change include the development of higher standards of education, social welfare legislation, the end of the era of domestic servants, and the introduction and widespread use of electricity, television, radio, the telephone and the motor vehicle. All of these developments have affected both lifestyles and architecture.

At home in the Queensland bush; Lower Tent Hill, 1910

A dining room scene, possibly in Tryune *or* Saltbush Park, *Mackay area, Queensland, c. 1886.*

A view from a drawing room into a dining room, showing the use of curtains on the archway between. Mapleton, Queensland, 1900

THE HISTORICAL APPROACH

The authentic restoration of a Victorian or Edwardian house requires some understanding of the architecture, interior design, furnishings and social conditions of the period in which it was constructed and of the status of its first owner or occupant. No matter what its quality, each house should be respected for what it is. The workman's cottage or the rich man's villa are both honest statements of an important era in Australian history.

Although this book does not call for the restoration of more than the exterior and the primary living rooms of most houses, knowledge of the work performed and the pleasures enjoyed in the various other rooms provides a useful and interesting background against which rejuvenation can proceed.

Dining rooms and drawing rooms were almost universal in Australian houses of the Victorian and Edwardian periods. The major features of both of these rooms were the windows, the door and the fireplace. Their relationship to each other, and the placement of their furniture and fittings, followed rules which were evolved in Britain and carefully transplanted to the Antipodean colonies. Houses which were designed by architects followed these rules rather more carefully than those which were the product of the many enterprising speculative builders who were responsible for so much of Australia's housing. But even speculative builders tended to some extent to follow those practices which had been established half a world away. Many Victorian builders had learned their trade in Britain or had been taught in Australia by British builders. Few of them were innovators; they built what they knew the public would accept.

DINING ROOM

The size and shape of the room dictated the scale and placement of the major items of furniture, namely the dining table and sideboard. The ideal was attained only in the houses of the upper middle class:

A dining table is usually about three feet six to four feet wide . . . Taking the width at four feet, a space of one foot nine must be added on each side for people sitting at table. This gives a total width between the backs of the chairs of seven feet six

Design for a dining room for a well-do-do Victorian household, from the Australasian Builder and Contractors' News, *9 June 1888*

A South Australian drawing room, probably in Adelaide, photographed in the 1880s

inches. A three feet passageway on each side . . . gives a dimension of thirteen feet six inches clear of the projection of the chimney-breast. . . . Fifteen feet is a better size, and if length be added in proportion, any width between that and twenty-four feet is a clear gain. A dining-room twenty-four feet by thirty-two feet may be called a grand room. The best rule for proportion of length to breadth is probably about three to two. Thus a room about fifteen feet wide should be twenty feet long.[18]

As far as the furniture was concerned the English architect G Lister Sutcliffe considered the following arrangement to be the most desirable:

If the sideboard is opposite the fireplace, the mistress of the house is properly seated with her back to the fireplace, at the 'head' of the table; the origin of the latter arrangement being that the master is supposed to be in touch with the butler and the wine. The fireplace and the sideboard ought therefore to be placed on the end walls of the usual oblong room rather than on the longer side walls . . . . To allow for easy service around the table, the clear width of the room ought not to be less than 14 feet, but the question of cost often necessitates a narrower room.[19]

DRAWING ROOM

This was a room for the use of the ladies of the household, for sewing, reading, family conversations, musical performances and recitals and for the reception and entertainment of visitors.

The aspect of the drawing-room, which is largely used in all kinds of houses in the afternoon, should be sunny and cheerful. Nothing can be more cheerful and pleasant than to sit in a cool room and look out on to warm and bright sunlight without being affected by the direct rays . . . . The drawing-room admits of any number of recesses, alcoves, oriel or bay windows, all of which afford facilities for the company to form themselves into groups for conversation, etc.[20]

Two views of the same Brisbane drawing room, photographed c. 1893.

A Sydney bedroom, 1906. The panel of flowers beneath the cornice is typical of the decorative effects that may be uncovered with careful research

Drawing room, Mount Lyell, Tasmania.

BEDROOMS

The governing features are not only the one or more windows, the one or more doors, and the fireplace, but obviously the bedstead, the dressing-table, the wash-stand, and the wardrobe .... The standard bedroom is one for the accommodation of a married couple. It is the custom for the lady to use it also for dressing, a small adjoining dressing-room being provided for the gentleman.[21]

The nursery department should always be placed within a convenient distance of the bedroom of the parents. At the same time it should be effectually shut off from the rest of the house.... however fond people may be of children, there are times when the noise and unrest ... become wearisome ....[22]

SERVANTS' QUARTERS

The servants' quarters or 'offices' consisted of the kitchen, scullery, larder and pantry. These occupied the ground floor at the rear of the house and were well away from the rooms used by the employer and the family.

It is not, as some might suppose, that allowance has to be made for class feeling as between superiors and inferiors; it is simply that the family desire to enjoy freedom from interruption, and that the servants have the same objection to be unduly disturbed or overlooked.... there are classes of households in which no distinctions of social status have to be observed ... but even then the principle need not be ignored.[23]

With its fuel or gas stove, and its pine table and dresser, the kitchen was the hub of the servants' quarters. Furniture had to be plain, strong and serviceable. Shelves and

The bedroom of Robert Sticht, American manager of the Mount Lyell mine, Queenstown, Tasmania

A cast-iron stove, shelves, a simple dresser and, no doubt, a pine table — in a typical Australian kitchen, 1906

cupboards were preferred to drawers. 'The fewer drawers there are in a kitchen the better, as they are apt to lead to untidiness and accumulation of dirt. One good cupboard . . . should furnish all the storage-room required in the kitchen by the cook.'[24]

Immediately adjacent was the scullery, used for the rough preparation of foodstuffs prior to cooking, for cleaning fish, and preparing meat and vegetables for the pot. Plates, cups, dishes and pans were washed here after the meal. One or two sinks were provided for the purpose and, in smaller houses, a copper for the family washing. The scullery was often provided with a small stove which supplemented the main kitchen range.

The larder was originally a storage area where salted meat was put away in jars and covered with lard. It had to be cool, dry and well ventilated to provide suitable storage for uncooked meat, vegetables and other perishables. The name 'pantry' is derived from the Latin *panis*, meaning bread. It served also for the storage of pastry and perhaps milk and butter. Towards the end of the Victorian period the larder tended to become home for most foodstuffs, while the pantry was given over to the cleaning and storing of silver and glass, the task of a housemaid in most Australian homes. The pantry was the butler's domain in the few houses which could afford such luxuries.

> . . . the butler has charge of the silver, glass, cutlery and all the china except the plates and dishes; and proper appliances in the shape of sink, draining-board, and hot and cold water service must be provided . . . . Where the pantry is on the ground-level, not in the basement, the butler's bed-room should be in immediate communication.[25]

Advertisements for servants from The Age, *Melbourne, 9 January 1890*

Penghana, *Queenstown, Tasmania,*
photographed in 1916.

THE HISTORY OF A HOUSE

DETERMINING THE DATE OF CONSTRUCTION

Curiosity is not the only reason for trying to determine when a house was built. Such information can be useful in carrying out a restoration programme by providing a guide to the selection of the various items that have to be replaced. Knowledge of the approximate date of construction will often assist discerning restorers in their efforts to finish, furnish and decorate in the correct style and manner of the period in which a house was constructed. The methods outlined will provide a basic guide to construction dating.

STYLISTIC   This method is usually most accurately performed by architects with an interest in old houses as it requires a comprehensive knowledge of a wide variety of styles of construction. It can be misleading as houses were sometimes built to a fashion which had been in vogue ten or twenty years before.

LEGAL   In most cases this method will also be a matter for an expert. It involves research into title deeds and documents often dating back to the period when the land on which the house was built was first granted or sold by the Crown. Requirements for the registration and transfer of property vary widely from state to state in Australia but in most states solicitors will be able to assist. A carefully conducted enquiry may provide information on the date of construction of a building which is accurate to within a matter of months.

GUIDES AND DIRECTORIES   Directories were published for the state capitals and some of the major towns of Australia during the second half of the nineteenth century. Sands' Sydney directories are an excellent guide to construction dates of houses in all of the old suburban areas of Sydney. Published from the early 1850s through to the 1920s, the Sands' directories list suburbs, streets, street numbers, names of residents and often the name of the house.

Sands' directories were published very early in the years which were stamped on their covers. A house which first appears in, for example, 1884, was probably built in 1883. Directories may be consulted in the various State Libraries or in a specialist historical library such as Sydney's Mitchell Library.

DESIGN REGISTRATION   Cast iron and other metal objects which were made in the United Kingdom and the Australian Colonies between 1842 and 1883 may be stamped with a design registration mark which can be useful in determining the approximate date of construction of a building in which they are found. From 1884 onwards a registration number replaced the characteristic symbol which was current in the earlier period. This number can also be used to determine the date on which the design of an object was registered.

The registration of designs was intended to provide manufacturers with protection for the appearance or ornamentation of their products. Between 1842 and 1883 registered designs were protected for three years. The registration symbol carried coded information indicating the date on which the design was registered. Thus, metal objects bearing the symbol will have been made within three years of the registration date. Access to the coded information, published here for the first time in an Australian building-restoration book, can simplify the task of dating a building.

The numerical system which came into effect from 1884 provided protection for designs for five years. From 1907 manufacturers could obtain extensions which took the period of protection up to a total of fifteen years.

Semi-detached houses, Adelaide, c. 1900.

Design registration marks and numbers provide a useful but not infallible method of dating a building. This method's defects include the possibility that careless or unscrupulous manufacturers may have continued using a die beyond the legally permitted date; in the possibility of quite lengthy intervals between manufacture and installation in a building; or to objects being removed from the building in which they were originally fitted and placed in another.

The registration symbol or number may be found on timber, glass, earthenware, fabrics and wallpaper, as well as cast iron locks, grates and other metal objects which were marked to provide protection for the ornamental designs which decorated their surfaces.

Registration symbols or numbers may also be found on cast iron decoration or 'lace'. The Australian Archives Office in Canberra holds many cast iron designs which were registered with authorities in the various colonies prior to Federation.

OTHER METHODS   Construction dating is also possible where access can be obtained to original records of various authorities. Council ratebooks, if still surviving, are useful sources. Consideration should also be given to archives of State Lands Departments, water and sewerage authorities, gas or electricity authorities, electoral rolls and census returns. The name of the original occupant or owner will frequently be required in such searches.

Construction dating is seldom as easy as with this house in the Sydney suburb of Woolloomooloo

Cast-Iron Design Symbols for Construction Dating

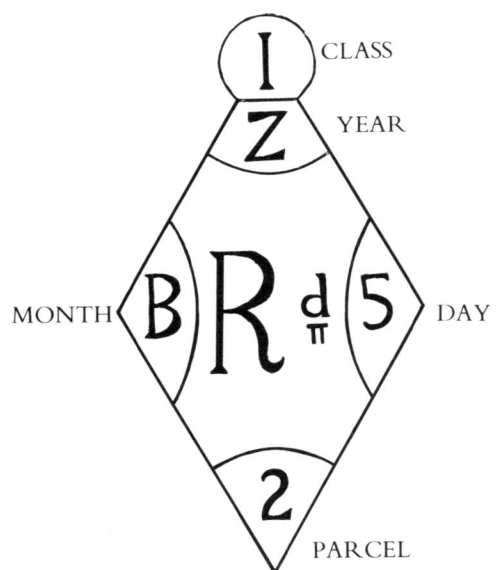

A design registration symbol set out in the pattern used between 1842 and 1867. The date encoded on this example is 5 October, 1860

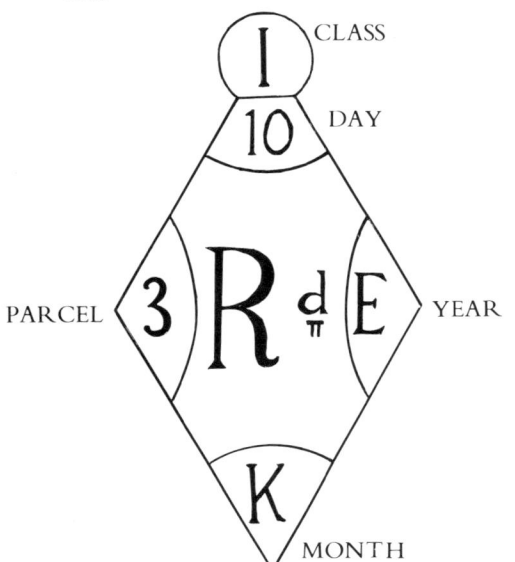

The date on this symbol, using the layout current from 1868 to 1883, is 10 November 1881

LETTER CODES FOR YEARS *1842* TO *1867*

Year code										
A	1845	F	1847	K	1857	P	1851	U	1848	Z	1860
B	1858	G	1863	L	1856	Q	1866	V	1850		
C	1844	H	1843	M	1859	R	1861	W	1865		
D	1852	I	1846	N	1864	S	1849	X	1842		
E	1855	J	1854	O	1862	T	1867	Y	1853		

Month code							
A	December	D	September	H	April	M	June
B	October	E	May	I	July	R†	August
C	January	G	February	K★	November	W	March

★ The letter **K** may be found as the month letter for December, 1860.
† The letter **R** may be found as the month letter for September 1–19, 1857.

LETTER CODES FOR YEARS *1868* TO *1883*

Year code										
A	1871	E	1881	I	1872	L	1882	U	1874	X	1868
C	1870	F	1873	J	1880	P	1877	V	1876	Y	1879
D★	1878	H	1869	K	1883	S	1875	W★	1878		

Month code							
A	December	D	September	H	April	M	June
B	October	E	May	I	July	R	August
C	January	G★	February	K	November	W	March

★ For March 1–6, 1878, the letter **G** was used for the month and **W** for the year.

NUMERICAL CODE FOR YEARS *1884* TO *1901*

Below are given the registration numbers with which each year commenced, on January 1. They relate not only to metal objects fitted to old houses, but to all types of materials for which designs were registered.

1	*1884*	116648	*1889*	224720	*1894*	331707	*1899*
19754	*1885*	141273	*1890*	246975	*1895*	351202	*1900*
40480	*1886*	163767	*1891*	268392	*1896*	368154	*1901*
64520	*1887*	185713	*1892*	291241	*1897*		
90483	*1888*	205240	*1893*	311658	*1898*		

Sunnybanks, *built by Thomas Grove at Middleton, Tasmania, in 1847, photographed c. 1889*

Beltana, *in the Hobart suburb of Lindisfarne, photographed by Charles Dairs c. 1900*

HOUSE NAMES

Houses built in the period studied in this book were normally named. These names have been lost in many cases, either as a result of changing fashions, or because the sheet of glass or metal plate which carried the name has been removed. It is often possible to re-discover a lost name and to make its replacement a part of the programme in which the original character of an old house is brought back to life.

The amount of time and thought devoted to the selection of a name for a house probably depended on its cost and the status of potential purchasers. It is unlikely that much thought was expended on names for speculative houses and it appears that fanlight glass, with names already etched into the decorative pattern, was bought from hardware merchants. The names of a row of terraces would have been bestowed at random; the sheets of glass being distributed along the row in the order in which they were unpacked.

Names were derived from many sources including international events, foreign and Australian cities, towns and places, flowers, birds, battles, famous people, rivers, mythology and so on. Increasingly, towards the turn of the century, Australian place names, aboriginal names and the names of native flora and fauna began to appear.

Names were changed from time to time to suit the fancy of a new owner. It is not uncommon for the same house to have had two or three names in the course of a century. However, where a name is embossed on the fanlight glass it can usually be accepted as the original name.

Where a house has lost its name, local directories of the period should be consulted. The absence of a house name from the relevant entry does not necessarily mean that the building did not have a name. Early entries for newly constructed houses were often erratic; the name may not have appeared in the directory for some years.

THE ARCHITECT OR BUILDER

It is sometimes possible to discover the name of the architect responsible for the design of a house and perhaps the identity of the builder who constructed it. Such information is more readily available in the case of the ambitious buildings which were the homes of the well-to-do of the period. However, well-known architects were often responsible for the design of terraces which were constructed by speculative builders for working-class and middle-class occupation.

A variety of sources can be consulted in carrying out research of this type. These may include directories, newspapers, and the various journals which circulated among architects, engineers, builders and contractors. Plans of early subdivisions, municipal records and the archives of authorities involved in the supply of water, sewerage, drainage, power and lighting may also be useful. A successful search for the name of the architect of a house may require the name of the original owner and the approximate date of construction. This information can be obtained in many cases from the relevant directories.

Once the year of first occupation has been established, it can be assumed that the building was constructed during the previous year. Procedures followed in arranging the construction of a house have changed very little since early last century. It was the custom then, as it is today, to seek tenders for the construction of all or part of a house by

Design for a house in Brisbane by Andreas Stombuco, c. 1888. Decorative cast iron is combined with the tall piers which were a major feature of Queensland architecture

advertising in the newspapers. If a house is known to have been first occupied in 1876 the search for tenders for its construction should begin six to twelve months beforehand. This will allow for the inevitable delays that occur in the process, unchanged since then, of obtaining a reasonable price and waiting for tradesmen, materials and good weather.

The search can begin among the advertisements in newspapers and extend if necessary to trade magazines and journals which published such notices. Probably the most useful source for the period from 1887 to 1895 is the *Australasian Builder and Contractors' News*.

The following selection from the 'tenders' notices indicates the type of information which is available in that journal:

> Adelaide. Erection of a pair of houses, Carrington-street. W. Anderson, Currie-street West, Adelaide, architect.   *September 1, 1894.*

> For erection of pair of villas (brick) in Grey-street, South Brisbane, J. B. Nicholson, architect, Brisbane.   *May 12, 1888.*

An Edwardian house in the Hobart suburb of Lindisfarne, photographed early this century

Not every entry is quite as specific and many simply call for tenders for a house or houses in an un-named part of a particular suburb, town or city. For example:

> Zillmere. Erection of dwelling. J. Hall and Son, architects, Brisbane.   *April 4, 1891.*

> Hobart. Erection of four cottages. R. J. Rogers and son.   *April 11, 1891.*

> Fitzroy. Erection of terrace of two-storey houses. Beswicke and Hutchins, architects, Melbourne.   *August 10, 1889.*

Success with this type of research is greatly facilitated when the names of the architect and owner appear, as in the following example of a successful tender published on October 12, 1889:

> Kew. Erection two storeyed brick residence and stabling in Sackville Street for W. H. Jarman, Esq., Peter Matthews, architect, Melbourne. Deposit £50.

	Residence	Stabling
A. G. Moore (ac.)	£2750	£196
Geo. Knox	£3005.16.2	£370

Research of this type depends as much on luck as on the perseverance of the restorer and the availability of the right source material. Most people should consider themselves well satisfied if they can discover the name of their house, its first owner and the year of construction. In undertaking a programme of building research the best approach is to adopt an attitude of hopeful pessimism. There are fascinating possibilities but disappointment is common.

The surrounds

Victorian and Edwardian architects and builders appeared to share an appreciation of the importance of the concept that we know today as streetscape, although it was not widely discussed. The lecturer Denis O'Donovan referred to it in 1872 when he told an audience in Melbourne that: 'Though all the buildings in a street should be by no means alike in size and design, a certain harmony should bind them all together.'[1]

FENCES

While individuality in housing was very positively expressed it was done within the framework of an overall cohesion which created a pleasant impression when the street was seen as a whole. Fences were clearly seen as an important element in the visual character of the street environment.

Cast iron was the principal material employed in fences and gates of the better quality houses. A typical palisade fence of the Victorian era consisted of vertical iron rods separated by horizontal elements of flat iron. The rods were set in a stone base with stone, brick or, occasionally, cast iron pillars to provide solidity and strength. The rods were

Cast-iron and stone create an imposing fence for a pair of houses in the Sydney suburb of Glebe. Middle-class homes were usually protected by cast-iron fences while timber pickets were usual for working-class houses

surmounted by the characteristic cast iron spearheads, in widely varying styles, which gave the fence its decorative character.

Working class cottages were usually provided with picket fences. Decoration came in the form of the various shapes used for the tops of the pickets and by sweeping the line of pickets upwards in a graceful curve towards the top of the posts which were located at intervals along the fence. More than thirty different patterns in picket fences have been found on the Federal Government's Glebe restoration project in Sydney.

More utilitarian and materialistic views in the twentieth century, coupled with the economic effects on homeowners and landlords of two world wars and the Depression, resulted in the demolition of many original fences. They were often replaced by squalid structures which contributed nothing to the character of the building and which diminished the appeal of the streetscape. Repairs to ageing cast-iron fences were considered to be too much trouble for not enough effect, although the latter was a very minor consideration. In more recent times the tendency has been to erect blank brick walls of up to two metres high. These are a regrettable effect of the increased noise level in our streets, combined with a misplaced zeal for privacy in houses which are already very private.

Designs for railing heads for cast-iron fences varied from state to state and at different locations within the states. This Edwardian house is in Drummond Street in the Melbourne suburb of Carlton

A terraced cottage in a suburb of Perth, W A

New picket fences from patterns used in the 1860s and 70s have been used on the Federal Government's Glebe restoration project in Sydney

SAXTON & BINNS, LTD.

HARDWOOD PICKETS.

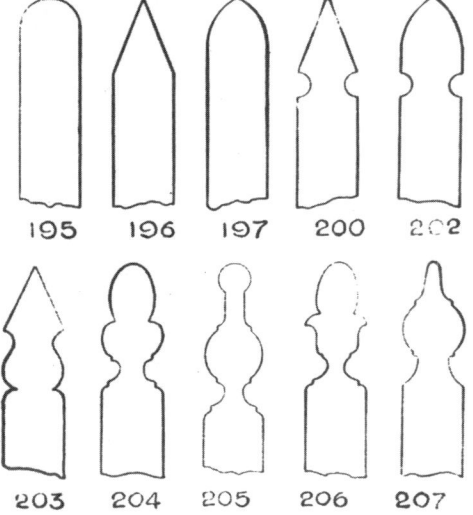

195   196   197   200   202

203   204   205   206   207

A page from the 1905 catalogue of the major Sydney builders' supply merchants, Saxton and Binns Ltd

Cast-iron palisade fences, stepped down the slope of a hill in the Sydney suburb of Paddington

Excessive traffic noise can be greatly diminished by a good growth of trees and shrubs in the garden, combined with the sound-absorbing qualities of carpet, soft furnishings and wall hangings. These can achieve much the same effect as a high brick wall on the street alignment and will not detract from the character of the street and the appearance of the house. Hedges, much favoured in Victorian times, will cut down street noise and help make the front garden a private place.

The repair or replacement of the original fence is an important aspect of any restoration programme. Repairs to damaged fences can usually be carried out without recourse to the skills of expensive tradesmen. Missing rods in an iron fence may be replaced with galvanised mild steel rods painted to match the rest of the fence. They may be set into the stone base by the use of a modern plastic glue or, preferably, by pouring molten lead into the hole around the rod as was done in the nineteenth century.

Missing or damaged spear heads may be replaced quite easily if the pattern is a stock

Modern reproductions of nineteenth-century railing heads are easily obtained, permitting the construction of new palisade fences which are indistinguishable from their Victorian counterparts.

Ellimatta, in Drummond Street, Carlton, Victoria, features an imposing cast-iron fence and cast-iron decoration which echoes the arches above its door and windows

line available from foundries or dealers specialising in cast-iron or aluminium reproductions of old cast-iron patterns. Where no suitable replacements can be found it may be necessary to have special castings made using one of the existing spear heads as a model.

If an old house has lost its original iron fence, it can be replaced in the same style without great expense or difficulty. Metal fabricators and welding shops will create the same effect in galvanised mild steel, using cast aluminium spear heads, providing a detailed plan is supplied. The fence should be in the same style and of the same height as those of adjoining or nearby houses with original fences.

The replacement of picket fences is primarily a matter of locating a timber yard or joinery which is prepared to cut pickets to the appropriate size and shape. A sample or a good detailed drawing should be provided. The construction of the fence is a matter of elementary carpentry.

New pickets to a Victorian pattern, Derwent Street, Glebe, N S W. More than thirty picket patterns have been found in the Glebe restoration project area

The garden of a Victorian cottage in the Sydney suburb of Neutral Bay

Lisson Grove, Hawthorn, Victoria

GARDENS

Nineteenth-century gardens in the Australian colonies were essentially English. The process of bringing neatness and order to what was considered to be a straggling, unruly Antipodean environment had begun with the earliest settlers. It continued throughout the nineteenth century and was clearly influenced by the large numbers of new immigrants from the British isles. Native trees and shrubs were rooted out and replaced by comfortingly familiar species from 'home' as the settlers struggled to turn an unwilling Australia into an English garden.

During a visit to Van Diemen's Land in 1846, Colonel Godfrey Mundy described the homes and gardens of some several hundred members of 'the humbler classes' on the outskirts of Hobart.

> . . . all or nearly all being separate dwellings, with a patch of neat garden attached, and with rose and vine-clad porches, reminding me of the south of England's cotter's★ homes. The extraordinary luxuriance of the common red geranium at this season makes every spot look gay . . . . The hedges of sweet-briar, both in the town gardens and country enclosures, covered with its delicate rose, absolutely monopolize the air as a vehicle for its peculiar perfume . . . . Every kind of English flower and fruit appears to benefit by transportation to Van Diemen's Land.[2]

The period of rapid expansion that occurred from 1850 onward resulted in the development of new suburban areas on the outskirts of the major settlements in each of the colonies. Near Sydney, the suburb of Glebe began to undergo more intensive development as its large estates were broken up due to the 1840s depression. B C Peck traversed the main thoroughfare, Glebe Point Road, and in his *Recollections of Sydney* described the gardens that he saw there in 1850.

★ A peasant who occupies a cottage belonging to a farm.

Derwent Street, Glebe, N S W

Lisson Grove, Hawthorn, Victoria

On each side of the road are pretty white villas, of freestone, many of them having neatly laid out gardens in front, the surrounding gum trees and brushwood being partially cleared away to make room for these mementoes of English ease and comfort.[3]

As new cottages, villas and terraces began to cover the landscape of Australia, gardens were laid out and planted with hydrangeas, gardenias, holly, lavender, daphne, privet, plumbago, rosemary, may, lilac and roses. Ivy, jasmine, honeysuckle, wistaria, clematis and bougainvillea began to climb the freshly painted cast-iron or timber columns of many smart new residences. Further away from the houses were planted trees such as ash, oak, chestnut, weeping willow, pepper, English elm, and the native Bunya Bunya, hoop pine, lemon-scented gum and Norfolk Island pine. Native ferns were popular and became a fashionable motif in architecture and decoration, particularly towards the end of the nineteenth century. The attempt to simulate a far-away homeland led to the release during the 1850s and '60s of English thrushes, starlings, blackbirds, skylarks, sparrows and rabbits.[4]

The health-giving role of plants and trees was recognised in Australia in the early 1870s as the increasing congestion in the major cities led to complaints about current forms of air pollution.

Trees, it must be remembered, are not only beautiful, but are highly conducive to health. They not only absorb the carbonic acid gas . . . but they also . . . appropriate large quantities of the noxious gases formed by the breathing of animals, the combustion of fuel, and the exhalations of sewers; and in return . . . they are constantly giving forth the pure oxygen, on which the salubrity of the atmosphere depends.[5]

As urban congestion grew the houses of the working classes in the larger towns and cities were left with little or no room for gardens. Some observers considered that this absence of garden space contributed to the poor moral tone which was considered to be the primary fault of the lower classes.

The garden and residence of Adye Douglas, Launceston, Tasmania, photographed c. 1870

A doctor's residence, Kingston, Victoria, from the Australasian Builder and Contractors' News, *25 February 1893*

Salt glazed urns, probably of colonial manufacture, in the garden of an Edwardian house in the Sydney suburb of Marrickville

Nothing can be more dreary than a house built close to others . . . without the sight of the smallest plant or flower. We shudder to think of it; and yet there are thousands of such houses in the State already. It is no wonder that the poor who live in such conditions lose interest, and gradually fall into conditions of squalid living and moral degradation.[6]

The lack of space for a garden eventually became one more excuse for the slum-clearers and moral agitators who, in the late nineteenth and early twentieth centuries, sought the demolition of entire inner-city suburbs of some of the major capital cities. Gardening, it was felt, contributed to moral improvement.

It is only necessary to observe the home life of the man who has a little garden about his house, to find out that in such cases there is domestic happiness, and better living conditions for his family. Fortunately such homes among the working classes are not absolutely rare, but they are too rare all the same, and if they could be made common a great influence towards the refinement and moral improvement of the people would result . . . .[7]

Authenticity in the restoration of a Victorian or Edwardian home calls for the creation of a garden appropriate to the taste and style of the period. This is a comparatively simple matter in the case of terraces and smaller cottages where the garden may be only a few square metres in area. Larger properties may pose more complex problems. The front garden of a large Victorian house may have had a carriage drive, fountain, pond and statues. Large trees and shrubs may be growing where once the carriages rolled, the pond may have disappeared, the piping for the fountain rusted beyond repair, and the statues either damaged or missing from their pedestals. With patience and energy, together with the aid of sympathetic and skilled tradesmen, anything can be repaired or replaced.

Garden edging tiles and chequered paving-bricks are important elements in the re-creation of a typical nineteenth-century garden. Garden edging tiles were among the range of salt-glazed ware produced by many Australian potteries prior to 1900. Decorative and yet highly practical, they were an earlier age's response to simple problems which are often solved today in a less appealing fashion. With their attractive raised patterns of flowers or simple, stylized shapes they retained the earth while bringing neatness and order to Victorian and Edwardian gardens. They added a touch of the adornment which was the joy of the age to what had been, not so very long before, part of the Australian bush. Australian potteries produced large quantities of garden edging tiles but few of them survive today.

The 1889 and 1895 catalogues of the Lithgow Pottery, N S W, contain three patterns for garden edging tiles. Each was 229 mm high by 146 mm wide (9 in × 5¾ in) and sold in 1895 for 12/- per hundred.[8] Garden edging tiles were easily broken by a careless blow from a spade or fork and were frequently discarded by unappreciative property owners.

Over the years most of them have been despatched to rubbish tips.

Where fragments are found in a garden they can be retained to indicate the pattern originally used and which ideally should be matched in the restoration programme. If reasonable numbers of unbroken tiles survive they should be carefully preserved and utilised to create the best possible effect. Finding replacements, especially in the same style, can be extremely difficult and may involve a long search in the gardens of houses under demolition. To the author's knowledge, none of the existing Australian potteries or brickworks is making these interesting examples of Victoriana.

Paving bricks, with their characteristic criss-cross pattern, were popular for creating garden paths before concrete became the almost automatic choice of homeowners and builders. They provided excellent adhesion, especially in wet weather, and were easily laid on bare earth or a bed of sand. Those produced by the Lithgow Pottery measured 241×121×51 mm (9½×4¾×2 in). The price in 1895 was £5-5-0 per 1000.⁹ Paving bricks may be obtained at demolition sites from time to time or from Gulson's brickworks, Goulburn, N S W. The firm's address and telephone number is listed in the Directory, page 130.

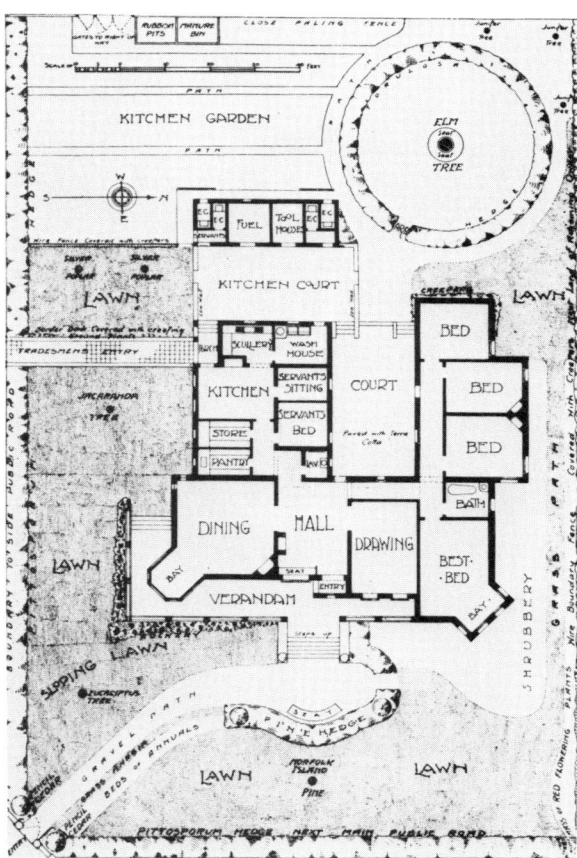

'The plan of a moderate-sized villa garden.'
Plate XLI in Robert Haddon's 'Australian Architecture' 1905

Two nineteenth-century paving bricks and a selection of salt glazed garden edging tiles. The tiles in the middle, L to R, are by: 1. possibly Mashman Bros., 2. Lithgow, 3. 4. Gulson's of Goulburn

Structure

Drummond Street, Carlton, Victoria

The suburbs and towns of Australia contain an architectural and historic treasury; buildings which in their masonry, cast iron, timber, plaster and ceramics contain the story of an era and of a nation in the process of formation. When young Victoria became Queen in 1837 the concept of Australian nationhood was a wild dream—the hopeless cause of a few colonial radicals. At the close of the period covered by this book Australia was a nation, although still very firmly bound to Britain. This chapter on structure begins with brick and stone.

MASONRY

Brick was the most popular basic building material in Australia in the period covered by this book. Other materials may dominate when one area or state is considered in isolation. Queensland houses, with their reliance on timber, are an obvious example. Prior to about 1870 bricks were handmade in a mould or stock which was lined with sand to enable easy removal after baking. These are commonly known as sandstocks. The introduction of mechanisation to the Australian brick manufacturing industry during the 1870s and 1880s and the progressive achievement of technological improvement resulted in a gradual increase in the quality of local bricks and the availability of a wider range of brick types.

Stone was popular from the early colonial period but its price was seldom competitive with that of brick. Although stone and brick were available in a wide range of types and varieties the builder's choice was often limited in practice. The builders of Sydney used local sandstone for the footings of domestic buildings and for the bases and piers of fences. Basalt, generally known as bluestone, was widely used in Melbourne.

'Craven's patent brickmaking machine.' The Building, Engineering and Mining Journal *reported on 28 July 1888 that 'several of these machines are already in use in these colonies'. It was said that the machine could make 10 000 bricks per ten-hour working day*

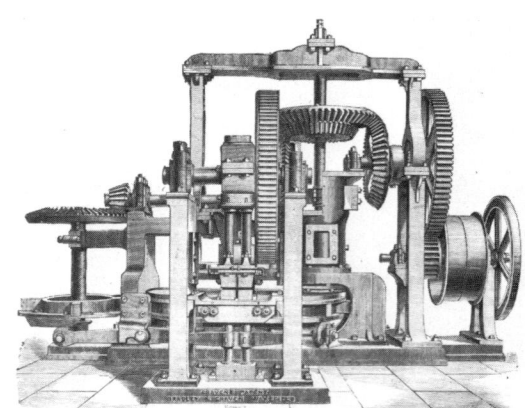

*From the subdivision plan of the Campsie
Park Estate, N S W, 1885*

In lands of sunshine architecture admits of a delicate relief of surface and moulding
which gives it a charm unknown in gloomier climes, but such details would be lost
upon our basalt; minute embellishments would be unseen, and the shadows absorbed
to a great extent. Its cheapness and durability, however, are qualities not to be
despised . . . .[1]

Other popular stones used in Victoria in the nineteenth century included Oamaru limestone from New Zealand and Barrabool Hills sandstone from near Geelong. They were
not compatible, although often used together, and many cases of deterioration have
resulted from lime washing into the sandstone.

Australian building stones were formed by volcanic action, the deposition of sediment,
or by the action of heat and pressure on sedimentary rocks. Basalt and granite are the
most commonly used of the volcanic or igneous rocks. Sandstone and limestone belong
to the sedimentary group and are the softest and most vulnerable stones used in building.
The metamorphic group, formed from sedimentary rocks, includes marble and slate.

CAUSES OF DECAY

Brick and stone, and indeed all traditional building materials, are subject to attack from
a variety of sources. Deterioration and ultimate decay will result unless the source of
attack is understood and dealt with. This process of gradual breakdown is part of the
natural order of things. It may not be possible to prevent it but it can usually be slowed
down. In many cases problems with stone are due to innate defects. Stone taken from
near the top of a quarry was often weathered and unsound. Stone from different quarries
could vary greatly in quality, appearance and durability. The three quarries in the Sydney suburb of Pyrmont in the nineteenth century were known as Heaven, Hell and

Plate R from R S Burn's New Guide to
Masonry, Bricklaying and Plastering

*Stone cottage at 42 Goldsmith Street,
Goulburn, N S W. Its simplicity suggests a
construction date before 1850*

The effects on masonry walls of climbing
plants such as ivy may be either detrimental or
beneficial, depending on the plant and the
circumstances. Ivy's aerial roots may damage
soft mortar. Climbers can protect walls from
moisture and provide added insulation against
extremes of temperature.

Purgatory—names awarded by the quarrymen and masons who had rated the degree of
ease, or hardship, with which they could be worked.

Dust and other abrasive material blown by the wind can abrade stone over long
periods. One of the major causes of breakdown of brick, stone and mortar is moisture
laden with salts from the ground or from cement. The moisture evaporates from the surface of the masonry, leaving the salts behind to form crystals that flake away the surface
of the brick or stone. For this reason it is essential to use a mortar that is softer than either
the stone or brick in which it is to be used. As water always follows the easiest path it
will tend to move into the soft mortar and evaporate from there.

The mortar may eventually have to be replaced but repointing is cheaper and easier
than replacing either stone or brickwork. It is important that the replacement mortar
be mixed and applied in such a fashion that it matches adjacent old mortar. The use of
lime mortar is recommended. One part of rock lime should be mixed with three parts
of water in a tank for a minimum of two hours and stirred from time to time throughout this period. Contact with the lime should be avoided. The mixture is then sieved
into another receptacle, drained and allowed to cool. The slaked lime is mixed with
sharp, clean sand in a ratio of one part of lime to three of sand. Weaker mixes of one
part of lime to six or seven parts of sand, together with a pinch of cement, are also
used.

Stone buildings were usually lime-plastered on the inside and it is not advisable to remove this plaster unless it has been affected by damp. The stonework beneath the plaster
was never meant to be exposed to view and for that reason it will appear crude and unattractive. On this point, as on so many others, the intentions of the builders should be
respected. Stone or brick walls which have been saturated with salts accumulated as a
result of many years of rising damp may need to be decontaminated before they are
replastered. Brushing the walls down or washing them with water may remove enough
of the salts to permit replastering in safety. In England, Attapulgus clay is used to form
a poultice which helps to remove salts from masonry walls.

Problems may also occur where stone has been used in conjunction with materials

with which it is not compatible. Cast iron or steel used in fences with stone foundations and piers may cause cracking and rupturing of the stone due either to rust or to the expansion and contraction of the metal. The problem is less likely to occur where lead wrapping or molten lead has been used as a buffer between the stone and the harder metal. Where severe cracking has occurred it may be necessary to replace the stone and the advice of an experienced stonemason should be sought. The new stone should be protected from any further splitting resulting from metallic expansion. Replacement steel used in conjunction with stone, or any other material, should always be well galvanised.

Restoration experts, faced with the problem of replacing badly deteriorated stone-work in a building, attempt to match the existing stone in colour, shape and overall appearance. New sandstone can be coloured to match old stone by painting it with water in which cow droppings have been left to soak for four hours. The droppings are sieved out and the residual liquid is applied with a brush. Stonemasons also used tea-leaves to obtain a similar effect.

Silicon esters have been used in Europe for several decades to consolidate flaking and deteriorating stone. Their use in Australia has not been extensive and conclusive information on their effectiveness and durability is lacking. One of these, ethyl silicate, is available from a supplier listed in the Directory, page 131.

If stone is to be cleaned nothing more than water and a soft brush should be used. Sandblasting or the use of high-pressure water jets to clean or remove paint from stone or sandstock bricks is not recommended as there is a risk of pitting and wearing away the surface. Needleguns, available from firms which hire out building equipment, are useful for removing paint from stone and brick.

RISING DAMP

Rising damp is perhaps the most troublesome and most common problem in old houses of brick or stone. Its presence is usually indicated by discoloured wallpaper or by a network of bubbles rising from the surface of the plaster, by a musty smell or rotting skirting

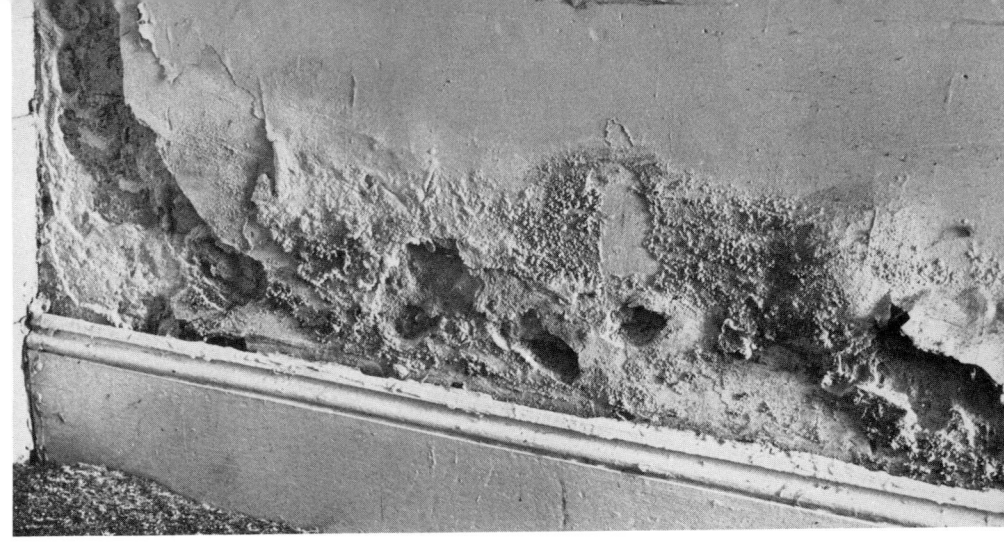

The effects of severe rising damp, untreated for many years

boards. The cause is invariably failure of the dampcourse—the barrier, often of slate or lead, which was intended to prevent groundwater being absorbed into the walls of the house. Many Victorian speculative builders failed to install dampcourses due to ignorance or as one method of cutting costs. Although the need for dampcourses was widely recognised by the 1860s, houses were still being built without them in Australia as late as the 1880s. Victorian builders who deliberately omitted dampcourses were among our earliest and most successful jerrybuilders. The effects of their malpractice were usually not evident for many years.

There is no simple, easy or cheap cure. A variety of methods is currently used to tackle this problem but some of them are of questionable value. It appears that the most effective and lasting solution, though not necessarily the easiest, is the traditional one: insert a metallic strip into the wall, as close to the foundations as possible. The metal strip or sheet must pass through the full thickness of the wall and it must be below the level of all flooring timbers. Water is an insidious liquid and is capable of slowly destroying or causing the deterioration of most common building materials.

It is possible to spend a great deal of money on overcoming the problem of rising damp. It is also possible to achieve the objective comparatively economically. The methods used will vary greatly and depend on the extent and nature of the problem in individual houses.

The initial approach to the problem in all cases is the same; affected plaster must be stripped from the wall to expose bare brick to a height of approximately half a metre above the level of the bubbles. The presence of moisture over a long period of time has resulted in the accumulation of salts, usually chlorides or sulphates, in this plaster. These will absorb moisture from the atmosphere during wet or humid weather even if all rising damp is stopped. The exposed brickwork should be left bare for six months after a new dampcourse is fitted to allow the wall to dry out. Skirting boards should be removed from damp areas and may have to be renewed if badly affected.

The principal methods used to combat rising damp are as follows:

INSERTION OF NEW DAMPCOURSE   This is the traditional approach and the method that is generally recommended as having stood the test of time. Most hardware stores now stock the coated aluminium or polyethylene strips which are currently used for this purpose. The Commonwealth Experimental Building Station recommends the use of 20 kg lead (4 lb), an opinion that is endorsed by many architects and builders. Lead is considerably more expensive than aluminium or plastic. Modern lead has less impurities than that which was formerly used for building purposes and is not as durable when used for dampcoursing.

Whatever the material chosen, the installation of the new dampcourse is a job that can be done by the owner. It is normally a difficult and arduous task and it may be best to seek a skilled bricklayer who is willing to take it on. First, a coarse saw or thin scraper

Coolooli, a brick house on a stone base at West Hobart, photographed c. 1912

is used to remove the mortar from between the joints in the brickwork. The selected dampcourse is then inserted and fresh mortar rammed into the remaining space. The maximum length of mortar that should be removed at any one time is a metre, as the risk of settlement increases beyond this length. Lengths of dampcourse should be overlapped by at least 150 mm to ensure that the water barrier is fully effective. A variation of this method, and the one normally used by bricklayers, is to remove one or two courses of bricks from the wall for the full extent of the affected area. This provides easier access and simplifies the task of fitting the dampcourse.

Several days work by a good bricklayer should be enough to fit a new dampcourse to most houses, ending the problem of rising damp for many years at least.

ELECTRICAL METHOD This process, commonly known as electro-osmosis, has been used in Australia for some years.

In active electro-osmosis, rows of electrodes are placed in a damp wall and a direct current potential is applied between them. Water migrates down from within the wall to the lower row of electrodes, eventually reducing or eliminating dampness in the upper part of the wall. Its disadvantages, apart from any current scientific questioning of its effectiveness, include the continuing cost of electricity and the corrosion of the electrodes.

The passive system uses a continuous copper strip which is grouted into a row of holes near the base of the damp wall and connected to earthing rods which are driven into the ground. It is said that this creates a short circuit which eliminates the potential difference associated with the rise of moisture by capillary action. Critics claim that where this system appears to be successful the results achieved are due largely to the various activities associated with its installation. Plaster is renewed and eventually repainted, new skirting boards may be fitted, and underfloor ventilation is increased. The factors involved in many houses where rising damp is a problem are often delicately balanced and slight changes in the building environment can have a considerable effect. In situations where the damp problem is not especially severe it may be years before new plaster begins to fail. The electro-osmotic system of halting rising damp has been tested in Australia by the C S I R O and the Commonwealth Experimental Building Station and, in the United Kingdom, by the Building Research Establishment.

Improved underfloor ventilation is often useful in combating rising damp. Ventilators should be installed to provide a good cross-flow of air throughout the underfloor area of the building and so increase evaporation. Cast-iron ventilators may be preferred for use in prominent locations on old houses. Improvements to drainage can also assist in alleviating rising damp.

The Bertrams, at the corner of Byron Street and Fitzroy Place, Hobart, photographed in the 1880s

47

The effects of weathering on masonry,
cast-cement decoration and timber,
Drummond Street, Carlton, Victoria

PLASTERER'S 'CURE'   This simply consists of replacing affected plaster with new plaster or cement render to which a water-proofing compound may have been added. No effort is made to prevent water from entering the wall; it is merely prevented from rising to the surface of the plaster or render. A common effect of this technique is to drive the water further up the wall so that it eventually moves above the level of the new surface and appears far higher than before. It is a short-term solution only and one that invariably proves very costly in the long run.

EVAPORATION TUBES   The technique of inserting evaporation tubes, known in Europe as the Knapen system, relies on increasing the evaporation of moisture from damp walls. Porous tubes of ceramic or other material are inserted into holes drilled slanting upwards into the wall above ground level and below the flooring timbers. Research on this method indicates that in many cases its effectiveness is limited and better results may be obtained by simply drilling unlined holes into the masonry.

CHEMICAL INJECTION   A series of holes is drilled into the wall from both sides, close to the ground and beneath the level of the joists and bearers. A water-proofing chemical is then pressure injected into the holes and spreads throughout the wall to form a continuous barrier to rising damp. The interval between the holes varies, depending on the chemical selected and the opinion of the company or individual operator. However, 10 cm is a common distance between holes.

The effectiveness of this method depends to a large degree on the thoroughness with which the application is performed. The durability of the various chemicals used, under conditions of heat, cold and moisture over a period of years, is also largely unknown. Insufficient chemical or over-large intervals between holes may provide gaps in the water-proofing barrier through which the damp will continue to rise. Where a wall of stone or brick contains cavities, either within the bricks or between the stones, the chemical may tend to fill these cavities and its dispersal and effectiveness as a barrier to damp will be limited.

Formulations used for this process include solvent-based silicones, aluminium stearates, water-based siliconates, and mixtures of rubber latex and siliconates.

Despite its limitations and some questions which remain about its effectiveness over a long period of time, chemical injection is clearly one of the most interesting new developments in the building industry's efforts to combat rising damp. An increasing number of companies can be expected to offer chemical injection damp proofing services to homeowners. Competition may result in a lowering of the present high prices demanded for this service.

Homeowners can install their own chemical damp course at comparatively little expense. The Dow Corning company manufactures a suitable product, Drisil 48, which is available from chemical suppliers. The major tool required is an electric drill with a 5 mm bit. Two holes should be drilled in every brick in the same course, on both sides of the walls. Holes are angled down to ensure that the chemical will flow in. In cavity walls the brickwork should be penetrated to a depth of approximately 85 mm in a brick of the normal width of approximately 100 mm. Solid brick walls of 230 mm thickness should be drilled to a depth of approximately 160 mm. Holes on opposite sides of the wall should be staggered to ensure maximum dispersal of the chemical. A funnel can be used to pour the chemical into the holes or a suitable pump can be hired. The bricks should be well saturated with the chemical before the holes are filled with mortar.

TIMBER

There was little demand for timber for building purposes in Australia during the first decade of young Queen Victoria's reign. The depression of the late 1830s and early 1840s caused a severe slump from which the building industry did not fully recover until the boom years that followed the gold rushes. The period of unprecedented development that occurred between 1855 and the late 1880s, as the principal towns of the various colonies were transformed into capital cities, created intense demand for timber of both Australian and imported species. E W Rudder, an early settler on the Macleay River, claimed in February, 1838, that more than a million feet of cedar had been shipped from the River in the previous twelve months.[2]

TYPES OF TIMBER USED

Many different timbers were in common use between 1840 and 1910. The most widely used included Australian cedar, Kauri, Baltic pine, Oregon, Californian Redwood, local hardwood and the various species of native pine. Timber getters were frequently far in advance of the surveyors and explorers who carried out the official exploration of Australia. Although they left few records it is probable that they provided the popular names by which many well-known Australian timbers are known today.

They were as a whole a wild and ruthless bunch, guilty of atrocities that are hinted at but seldom described in the early records of the colonies. In 1838 cedar sawyers operating on the Macleay River, on the central coast of New South Wales, were described as 'lawless banditti' who terrorised the settlers and plied their convict servants and stockmen with illicit grog.[3]

A bush sawmill near Nerang, Queensland, from the Building, Engineering and Mining Journal, *29 December 1888*

A Melbourne timber merchant's advertisement in the Victorian Contractors' and Builders' Price Book, *1859*

A lone cedar tree, photographed in New South Wales at around the turn of the century

In *Our Antipodes* Colonel Godfrey Mundy described the activities of a gang of timber getters at The Cascades settlement, near Port Arthur in Tasmania, early in 1851:

At this place about 400 convicts are stationed, most of them being employed in felling timber, of which there is an endless supply of the largest size and finest quality near at hand. Alongside the wharf a fine brig, the Vigilant, was loading with spars and planks for England; including some splendid specimens of blue gum for the Admiralty. The longest plank on board was 94 feet in length, 4 inches thick and 16 inches wide. There were three or four spars upwards of 70 feet long by 2 feet thick. Some lying under water ready for use were, I was told, upwards of 100 feet long. I also saw in the hold of the brig some immense logs of 'light wood,' a non lucendo, darker than mahogany; and knots of the beautiful Huon pine, finer than bird's eye maple for ornamental furniture.

This wealth of colonial timber was used to considerable effect by nineteenth-century builders. Colonel Mundy was particularly impressed by the use of cedar in the houses of Sydney:

It has all the beauty in colour and figure of the Spanish mahogany . . . . In solidity and closeness of grain, the Australian cedar is, however, greatly inferior to mahogany. The doors, sashes, window-frames, and shutters, staircases and balustrades, skirting-boards and cornices . . . are of cedar. This profusion of dark-coloured unpainted wood . . . pleased my eye exceedingly; but my taste was disputed by many—some going so far as to assert that it made a dwelling-house look like a London gin-palace![4]

So plentiful was the supply of cedar that this superb timber was often grained to resemble other woods.

Use on this scale could not last and by 1891 there was belated official awareness that supplies of cedar were fast running out. J H Maiden, curator of the Sydney Technological Museum, told the Sydney Architectural Association of concern at the depletion of native cedar: '. . . the Forestry Department has found it necessary to undertake an extensive system of re-planting it, with the view to meet the requirements of the next and succeeding generations.'[5]

The project was a failure. The cedar twig borer flourished when cedar was grown in large stands, with trees in close proximity to one another. The artificially-planted cedar forests were decimated. A few cedar trees remain in rugged and isolated areas along Australia's east coast. But as far as the day to day trade of sawmills and timber yards is concerned Australian cedar is extinct.

As cedar became scarce and more expensive in the 1880s and 1890s efforts were made to find suitable replacements. Californian Redwood was an acceptable compromise, offering a similar appearance to cedar at a reasonable price. Pine, stained, varnished or grained to resemble more expensive timbers, was also used for architraves and skirting-boards. It had been a popular timber in the Australian building industry since before 1840. The most popular pines were Baltic and Kauri.

Baltic pine was imported from Northern Europe where the principal source of supply was Norway. James Nangle described it as

. . . a whitish, and slightly reddish yellow coloured timber, exceedingly pleasant to work, fairly strong and tough, and durable if not put in exposed positions. In, or

about Sydney, it is used only for joinery work such as window frames and sashes and doors, but in Melbourne it is used very extensively for all kinds of joinery, skirtings, architraves, etc.[6]

Baltic pine was a popular flooring timber for many years. Its major rival in this field was Kauri. Most of the Kauri used in Australia was imported from New Zealand although some was obtained in Queensland and Western Australia. Fine grained, free from knots and whitish yellow in colour with an unusual silky lustre, Kauri was highly regarded as a timber for joinery and flooring purposes. The use of Kauri and Baltic pine for flooring in Australian houses ended many years ago. Other species, more resistant to attack by borers and white ants, have been adopted by the timber industry.

The dimensions, as well as the species, have also changed. Floor boards, invariably 146 mm (5¾ in) wide in late Victorian and Edwardian Australia, are now normally much narrower. The largest boards readily available for flooring today are cut from 140 mm (5½ in) planks, producing a finished tongue and groove board 133 mm (5¼ in) wide. The modern timber industry's reliance on species that were not used for flooring in Victorian and Edwardian times, together with the vogue for narrow planks, makes restoration more difficult when floors must be replaced.

REPLACING FLOORING

The approach to the restoration of flooring will depend on the degree of damage to the existing floor. Where only a few boards are damaged it may be possible to take replacements from rooms where the floor is to be carpeted. The task becomes more difficult in circumstances where severe borer attack or the effects of damp indicate that the replacement of large areas, or the whole of the floor, is necessary.

Where the entire floor is to be replaced, the opportunity can be taken to improve the existing system of underfloor supporting timbers, to improve ventilation and to attack at the source any problems caused by the presence of rising damp. Once the defective flooring has been removed and all rubbish and debris has been cleared away it will probably be found that inadequate underfloor support has been provided by the original builder. 'Bouncing' floors are usually a reliable indicator of this. The problem is usually due, not so much to skimping on the part of the builder or architect although this may be part of the story, but to the comparative lack of knowledge of building engineering at the time of construction.

In most Australian states today the accepted standard is to frame the ground floors of domestic buildings in hardwood, using 100 × 75 mm bearers and 100 × 50 mm joists. Bearers are usually spaced at from 1300 mm to 1800 mm, and joists at 450 to 600 mm centres. Both span up to about 1800 mm, being supported by brick piers at least 230 mm square. In Queensland, greater spans are common and larger bearers and joists are then used. The South Australian practice is to place the joists on 75 × 25 mm timber, laid flat and supported by continuous brick walls 115 mm thick.

Hayling, *in the Sydney suburb of Hunter's Hill, dates from 1879*

A new floor for any part of the area to be restored in an old house should match adjacent floors both in the species of timber used and in the size of the boards. It is highly likely that the only source of supply will be demolition sites. While it is acceptable, for example, to replace a Baltic pine floor with one of Kauri the width of the planks used is quite important. In most cases floor boards narrower than 146 mm will be out of place in a house of the period in question.

Before flooring timber is purchased from a demolition site it should be carefully examined to ensure that it is free from borers. The timber should be examined from below, if fixed in place, or turned over if it is loose. If borer holes are found it would be wise to forego purchasing. Active borers can be detected by tapping the top of the board and, in a good light, watching for a fine dust which will fall from the holes in the under surface.

Kauri or Baltic pine flooring, or any other softwood species used prior to 1910, should be protected from heavy rain during the demolition process and should be stored under cover as soon as possible after removal. Experienced demolition contractors can lift an old floor far more easily, efficiently and with much less damage than any home handyman. In buying old flooring the area to be refloored should be calculated and from 10 to 20 per cent added to cover wastage.

Although the presence of nails and nail holes in second hand flooring may be a nuisance the use of this timber can result in a more acceptable floor at a lower price than the very cheapest modern flooring timber. The nails may be removed and the holes filled with putty stained to match the timber finish.

'Cupping' of the boards is the only other major problem likely to be encountered with second-hand flooring. This defect is usually an indicator of dampness under the floor. The underside of the boards gains moisture and swells, thus forcing the drier upper surface into a concave shape. The condition is easily detected by looking at the end of planks from slightly to one side. Moisture from any source will always damage flooring timber. Timber floors should therefore never be washed.

FLOORING FINISHES

Once all repairs to the floor have been made the question of the finish must be decided. The traditional approach was to paint the floor on the periphery of rooms with black japan. Original floors in most old buildings still carry the faded shadow of the black japan that was applied many years ago. This finish was used in entrance halls on the treads and risers of stairs, and around the bare, uncarpeted perimeters of dining and drawing rooms. The area painted depended on the size of the carpet square or rug which was to be used in the room. The black japan served to highlight, not the floor itself, but the floor covering. The black rim was the frame for a picture.

It is almost automatic today to have exposed timber floors fine sanded and finished with a commercial wax or plastic product which protects the timber but allows the grain to show through. The technology which makes this treatment possible is a comparatively recent development. It is therefore not appropriate in those areas of a house which are to be restored in strict accordance with historical principles. However, current attitudes towards floor sanding and finishing make it unlikely that the traditional process will again achieve widespread acceptance. For those members of the small, brave band who will insist on authenticity in this regard the names of Australian manufacturers of black japan are listed in the Directory, page 130.

Mr Clements' cottage at Avoca — see page 21

SQUEAKING FLOORS

This problem, a very common occurrence in old houses, can be corrected. It usually requires concentration and determination—factors which often relate to the degree of annoyance caused by the squeaks.

Squeaking is the result of movement and occurs when two boards rub together. It can be seasonal, resulting when the level of moisture in the air causes the boards to swell or shrink to the stage at which squeaking occurs. Typical causes of squeaking are:

○ Weakness in a board because of a defect, such as a large knot;
○ Too great a span between joists;
○ Excessive movement in bearers or joists due to a lack of packing for firm support, or to structural fault in these timbers;
○ Poor milling, producing loose-fitting tongues which give inadequate support to the board or boards when under load;
○ The use of damaged boards with broken tongues or missing bottom edges to the grooves.

The noise can be reduced by forcing a lubricant such as French chalk, wax or linseed oil down cracks in the vicinity of the squeak. This will normally provide relief from seasonally induced squeaking.

A permanent solution will involve the provision of additional support for affected areas. Where access can be gained to the underside of the floor, short lengths of joist can be inserted to support boards where excessive movement is occurring. The best means of discovering where the greatest movement is taking place is to go under the floor with a torch and carefully examine the area in which the squeak is occurring while someone walks back and forth across the affected area.

Where movement is visible a method of supporting the area should be provided. This may involve the construction of an additional pier or piers. Makeshift remedies, such as the insertion of a prop resting on a brick, are seldom satisfactory for long. A suitable pier consists of 230 or 280 mm brickwork resting on a concrete pad at least 150 mm thick, poured into a hole dug into firm ground.

WHITE ANTS AND BORERS

Serious damage can be inflicted on old buildings by the attack of insects such as white ants and borers. In restoration work it may often be found that infestations have occurred many years ago and that the work of the termites or borers has long since ended. In such cases action is limited to repair and replacement of affected timber and prevention of future attack.

Information and advice on white ants and the various species of borers may be obtained from State Forestry Departments, the Timber Development Association, the C S I R O's Division of Forest Products, members of the Timber Preservers' Association and major pest-control companies. The Commonwealth Experimental Building Station and the New South Wales Forestry Commission both provide excellent leaflets on white ants and borers. These cover identification, treatment and prevention of further attack.

Treatment of active infestations of white ants and borers may be undertaken by the property owner but the complexity of the treatment and the danger of the chemicals involved is such that the use of a professional pest-controller is recommended.

Timber shutters, Oddfellow's Hall, Darling Street, Balmain, N S W

Finishes

For many years old houses were despised in Australia. They were regarded as slums that should be demolished in order to make way for anything that was new. The present interest in them needs to be matched with knowledge of the intentions of their architects, builders and decorators. It is only through authentic restoration that the original character of old houses can be regained.

This chapter on finishes deals with some aspects that have frequently been destroyed or damaged or have suffered from deterioration over the years.

ROOFING

The roof should be the subject of one of the first, detailed inspections made when the condition of an old house is being assessed. It should be inspected from above and below in order to ensure that an accurate overall picture of its condition is obtained.

Large leaks will leave very positive indications inside the house. However, even where no evidence of leaking is seen from within the building, it is quite possible that there may be other problems which will only become apparent as a result of a close examination,

Shingled cottages in Flinders Street, Adelaide, photographed before 1890. The house on the left is suffering from severe rising damp

carried out from within the roof space. There is usually no other way of ensuring that a roof which appears from the ground to be in good condition will not begin leaking in a few months, perhaps after considerable expenditure on carpet, paint, wallpaper and furnishings.

SHINGLES, SLATES AND TILES

It is not advisable to venture upon a tile roof which is showing signs of age. If the roof is considered safe enough to walk upon, soft shoes should be worn and the line of the roofing battens should be followed by treading gently on the lower third of the tile. Ridge tiles should never be walked upon. Obvious faults will include cracked, broken, displaced or missing tiles or slates. Lead flashing around chimneys is often in need of replacement. It may be cracked or may have moved out of its crevice in the brickwork as soft mortar has weathered away. Patches of black, bituminous material on lead flashing or other parts of a roof indicates previous efforts to cure leaks, often without lasting success.

Inside the roof space the existence of leaks can be verified even in dry weather by shining a torch, not on the underside of the roof but on the top of the ceiling. Dripping water will leave a clean, washed hollow in the decades of dust and dirt that has accumulated there. A layer of this dust, on top of an old lath and plaster ceiling, will soak up a lot of water and conceal the existence of small leaks for long periods.

It should be borne in mind that the water may have trickled along one of the roof timbers for some distance before falling onto the ceiling. If so, it may have traced a path on the timber which will still be visible in dry weather. The precise location of leaks is best discovered during rain. When detected they should be marked with chalk or a felt-tipped marking pen to ensure quick and accurate location when repairs are being made.

Some compromises in renewing roofing materials may have to be made. The replacement of a perfectly sound modern roof of, for example, cement tiles with timber shingles or slate is an expenditure that few people would be prepared to make for the sake of absolute authenticity. Where an existing roof is to be replaced it is perfectly acceptable to fit corrugated iron as this material will place the building in a nineteenth-century context.

Where it is known that the present roof is not original it is of academic interest at least to be able to determine what type of roof first protected the building from the elements. In a few cases a modern galvanised iron roof will be found to conceal an original roof of shingles. Where a shingled roof has been completely replaced, broken shingles will usually be found scattered across the top of the ceiling. The same applies in the case of slate roofs. Fragments of slate will often also be found buried in the earth around the house.

Shingled cottages in Bent Street, Adelaide, c. 1870

Splitting shingles at a bush camp. From the Building, Engineering and Mining Journal, *15 December 1888*

Shingles, cut from the eucalyptus and casuarina (or she-oak), were the most common form of roofing material for most of the Victorian age. They were cheaper than slate but had a comparatively short life and substantially increased the risk of fire in a dwelling: 'The ideal roof covering, both as regards form and colour, is that made of thick split shingles, which soon acquire a silvery grey tone, which will harmonize well with anything. Shingles, unfortunately, cannot be used in the city, nor is it always practicable to use them elsewhere.'[1]

Galvanised iron roofing of various types was used from the 1840s. The firm of E C Weekes, ironmongers, advertised in *Sands' Sydney Directory* for 1866 that they could supply 'Galvanised Tinned Iron Tiles, for roofing, 90 lbs., 110 lbs., 130 lbs., to the square'. Builders had the choice of slate from South Australia, Wales or the United States. In 1908 Maxwell Porter, slater and slate merchant of Redfern, advertised his range as: 'Penrhyn Bangor, Portmadoc, Eureka Green, American Blue.'[2]

Slates, tiles and shingles each had their own bands of followers in the profession of architecture in late-Victorian Australia, though there were few who dared to praise galvanised iron:

> . . . a red-tiled roof (especially on a building of red brick) should never be used unless it is to be seen against a background of greenery. . . . in default of tiles of the right colour, slate approximating as near as may be to the colour of old shingles would seem to be the most suitable. Purple slates, and green, are not satisfactory if seen against the sky; and red slates are open to the same objection as red tiles, besides being less picturesque in appearance. Iron, of course, is the worst covering of all, because it is the most inartistic.[3]

Patterns on slate roofs were created with contrasting shapes and colours. They should be restored when the roof is repaired or replaced

Then, as now, there were almost as many opinions as there were architects—especially as the 1890s were a period of change in architecture. The new Federation style, with its emphasis on exposed red brick walls and red tiled roofs, was growing in popularity.

Slates were available in eight sizes of which the most popular were:

'Viscountesses	18" × 10"	200 to the square
Countesses	20" × 10"	171 to the square
Duchesses	24" × 12"	124 to the square'[4]

Patterns formed on the roof by contrasting shades and shapes of slates should be retained when an old slate roof is being renewed. The roof can be photographed or sketched to facilitate replacement of the pattern. A slate roof which is ready for repair or renewal lets individual slates slip, leaving gaping holes behind as they drop down into the gutter or garden.

Importation from France of the Marseilles terracotta tile in the early 1890s was a highly successful step by building merchants. Marseilles tiles gradually replaced slate and shingle and by the turn of the century had added a very distinctive new element to the landscape of urban Australia. Deterioration in a tiled roof is indicated by crumbling and cracked mortar beneath ridge tiles, by cracked tiles, loss of glaze and brittleness. When replacing old tiles demolition sites should be visited in order to obtain a close match in colour and appearance of age. Modern tiles are now made to metric sizes and will not fit into an old roof. However, manufacturers carry stocks of tiles which were made prior to metrication.

Recommended practice when re-roofing today, whether in shingles, slate or tiles, is for the use of sarking in all but roofs of high pitch. Sarking paper, silver on one side and blue on the other, provides both extra insulation and added protection from minor leaks.

GALVANISED IRON AND LEAD

> Aesthetically considered, this custom of roofing with galvanised iron is the most abominable abuse that has crept into colonial architecture.[5]

The opinion was that of James Nangle, an Australian authority on building construction, expressed in a lecture to the Engineering Association of New South Wales in 1895. Iron roofing, he believed, was suitable for large sheds, workshops and factories 'but not on a public, or domestic building of any permanence or importance'. This attitude towards galvanised iron developed towards the end of the Victorian era. It was a minority opinion; the great majority of builders and homeowners found galvanised iron to be a highly satisfactory roofing material. It combined practicality with efficiency, economy and versatility, achieving results and effects that no other roofing material could match. But in the houses of the middle class, where ambition sometimes outran means,

Marseilles tiles carried the rich redness of Federation-style houses up from the walls to the roof and reinforced the earthy warmth which was a feature of this Edwardian architectural fashion

Decorative ridge capping on a Federation-style house on the Sydney suburb of Haberfield. Slipping slates indicate the need for repairs

the humble sheets of iron were often banished to the rear; those planes of the roof which could be seen from the street were covered with the more costly and prestigious slate.

Iron was the wonder material of the British building industry in the eighteenth century. By 1840 the zinc-coating process had been developed to prevent deterioration of the metal caused by rust. In the 1850s roofing iron was being mass produced in thin, corrugated sheets coated with zinc. John Lysaght began to export large quantities from Britain to Australia where it was eagerly received in the cities, the towns and the bush. It was cheap, light, easy to transport and simple to apply.

Simon Zollner's 'Galvanized Iron Manufactory' began production in Sydney in 1863 and was soon turning out an extensive range of products including tanks, guttering, piping, ridging, hips and valleys. Zollner used imported galvanised sheet iron to produce the characteristic convex or concave shapes that became increasingly popular for the verandah roofing of a wide variety of housing types. In the six decades between the gold rushes and World War I, corrugated galvanised iron vied with and eventually replaced shingles as Australia's most popular roofing material.

Though slate, shingles or tiles could be used for the main body of the roof the curves which added interest to the roof of the balcony or verandah at the front of a house could be achieved only with corrugated iron. It simplified construction as curved sheets could easily span quite large distances. Correctly installed, corrugated iron was an extremely efficient roofing material, ensuring that not even the strongest of downpours was able to penetrate a house. There were never any airs or graces about corrugated iron but it was nevertheless the only material which could provide the particular effects required to set off the facade of the great majority of houses built in Australia before the turn of the century. By 1894 Lysaghts were shipping more than 40 000 tonnes to Australia every year.[6]

Fabricators provided Victorian and Edwardian builders with curves to suit any shape that they required. Simple suburban cottages were usually given a verandah roof of bull-nosed iron. In the last metre of the iron's downhill run the curve swept down abruptly to pour rainwater into the gutter with no risk of it overshooting. The curve was both practical and decorative, adding appeal to the use of a roofing material that in its bare

and unadorned state was too drab and uninteresting for the tastes of the majority of the Victorians and Edwardians. An alternative effect was obtained by forming the iron to imitate the droop of a canvas awning. This impression was reinforced by painting alternate sheets of iron in contrasting colours, often selected from colours used elsewhere on the building. Striping was also used to good effect on bullnosed iron.

In the period of from forty to sixty years in which inner-urban housing was degraded the original corrugated iron balcony or verandah roofing rusted through and its replacement became essential. In many cases the intention of the builders or architects was ignored and the appealing curve replaced by straight sheets of iron which contributed nothing to the appearance of the houses. It was a period in which form was sacrificed to function through sheer economic necessity or lack of appreciation. The well-organised system by which curved corrugated iron was provided to meet the needs of the builders of Victorian and Edwardian homes had, like the original iron itself, rusted away. The ordinary homeowner, faced with the problem of a roof which let in water at every shower, usually solved the problem by settling for the quickest, easiest and cheapest solution.

With the new interest in housing restoration it has become a simple matter to give old houses the verandah or balcony roofing shape which was such an important element of their original design. Most of the major cities have at least one supplier who is able to curve the iron to the shape required. In some cases, hardware stores located close to the area of greatest demand will have made arrangements with a sheetmetal workshop for flat sheets of corrugated iron to be rolled in accordance with a pattern or template supplied by the individual customer. Manufacturers of corrugated galvanised iron watertanks are usually able to assist.

A template ideally should consist of a sheet of the rusted curved iron that is to be replaced or one of the purlins or roof timbers used in some circumstances to support the iron. Where neither is available the shape of the original roof line may still be discernible as a faint pattern on the paint, in different degrees of fading on unpainted brickwork, or in the original lead flashing which is often left intact when a bullnosed roof is replaced by straight sheets of corrugated iron.

James Nangle wrote in 1895 that corrugated iron had 'become so generally used that it is seldom we see a building that has not some portion of it covered with this material'. The traditional bullnosed shape seen here is easily obtainable

The concave shape of this verandah roof, together with its striped paintwork, gives the impression of a canvas awning. T A Sisley criticised such roofs in 1890, saying 'the tinkling of rain or hail upon them is intolerable to such as are not callous to everything but beef and beer'.

New galvanised iron must be degreased before painting or the paint will begin to flake off quite quickly. The manufacturing process leaves an invisible greasy film on the surface to which paint cannot adhere. The iron should be thoroughly washed with a commercial degreasing agent or mineral turps before being painted with a coat of galvanised iron primer. Succeeding coats of paint should be applied in accordance with the manufacturer's instructions.

Lead is an important minor material commonly used in aspects of the roofing of old Australian houses. Strips of heavy lead are frequently to be found serving as ridge capping where a bullnosed corrugated-iron verandah-roof turns a corner. Our early builders acknowledged lead's unique suitability for this role which requires a considerable degree of malleability. The ridge capping had to be formed, for reasons both aesthetic and functional, so that it flowed into the hollows of the corrugated iron while following the bullnose curve down into the gutter. The fact that each application was unique as a result of variations in the position of the corrugations in the roofing iron ensured that no ready-made ridge capping could be used. It was customary to provide a graceful touch to a largely functional item of roofing by rolling the lead to form a shape that approximated to two-thirds of a circle. This roll usually stopped abruptly some 180–200 mm above the gutter.

Lead ridge-capping, formed in its traditional shape, has a particular character which adds an important detail to the restoration of an old house. The replacement of the lead, where it has deteriorated or been removed, is comparatively simple. Lead flashing, available at most hardware retailers, is ideal for the task. The width normally used is from 250–300 mm and the minimum weight of lead advisable is 15 kg.

The point where the two planes of the iron roof come together will be supported by a purlin, curved to the shape of the bullnosing. Short lengths of thick dowelling are attached to the top of the purlin above the roof by nails or screws which either slip through the gap where the iron meets or pierce the edge of the iron. The dowelling used should be approximately 30–40 mm thick—sizes which are not normally carried by tim-

ber yards or suppliers. They may be available from specialist joiners or can be run off as a special order by an obliging joiner or timber merchant. Thinner dowelling is not appropriate.

The dowelling should be cut into short lengths, with the cuts made so that each piece of dowel meets with its neighbours closely and neatly. The intention is to give the impression of a continuous, curved piece of dowelling. The whole line of short pieces of dowel should be firmly fixed and carefully follow the shape of the bullnosed iron, stopping at about 180–200 mm above the rim of the gutter. In the case of simple cottages it is often continued into the gutter.

When the dowelling has been fixed in place, the lead is cut to length and slipped under the flashing at the point where the roof departs from the main structure of the building. It can be attached here by one or two brass screws and brass washers, or by copper nails or long copper tacks, which are inserted into the dowelling. It is important to ensure that the screws or tacks will be covered by the flashing when it is replaced. Except in long runs of lead ridging, no further means of fixing the lead should be necessary although it may be tucked under the corrugated iron where the iron ends in or just above the gutter.

The lead, carefully moulded by the use of the traditional wooden lead-working mallets, should closely follow the shape of both the dowelling and the curves and corrugations of the galvanised iron. It will be held in place by its own weight. Lead that is too firmly fixed by an excess of screws or tacks at various points along its length cannot expand and contract in extremes of temperatures and will be liable to distortion and eventual cracking as a result of metal fatigue.

Recent research carried out in London has resulted in a recommendation by the Lead Development Association that the maximum length of lead sheet used as cover flashing should be no more than 1·5 m when fully exposed to the sun. However, longer lengths appear to have been used successfully as ridge capping in Australia for many years without serious problems from distortion or fatigue. The lead is moulded to the required

shape by a gradual process which involves the repetition of many gentle taps with the wooden mallet. Particular care should be taken in the formation of the shape at the point where the dowelling comes to an abrupt end; it is very easy to tear the lead at this point.

Lead has high resistance to atmospheric corrosion and forms a highly insoluble patina that will not stain or harm associated materials such as stone or galvanised iron. It can be used in close contact with other metals such as copper, zinc, iron and aluminium without stimulating electrolytic corrosion. However, lead in contact over a long period of time with damp timber is likely to be slowly corroded as a result of the action of acids leached from the wood. Western red cedar and hardwoods are particular contributors to this form of attack. Concrete made from portland cement contains free alkali which can stimulate a slow corrosive attack on lead in the presence of moisture.

Further information on the use of lead in roofing is to be found in the publication *Lead Roofing*, published by the Lead Development Association, 34 Berkeley Square, London, and available in Australia from the Broken Hill Associated Smelters, 95 Collins Street, Melbourne 3001.

GUTTERING, DOWNPIPES AND DRAINAGE

The provision of a properly functioning system to carry rainwater from the roof out into the street is an important element in the overall programme of upgrading and improving an old house. The efficiency of a good roof can be nullified if leaking gutters, downpipes or drainage lines discharge water into the walls or foundations of a building. A thorough examination, both from the ground and on a ladder, is the first step. Rust can be raging away beneath a coat of paint on what from the ground appears to be a perfectly sound piece of galvanised iron downpipe or guttering. Leaking or rusty guttering and down-pipes should be replaced as soon as possible.

It is not commonly realised that guttering, as with so many other items used in domestic buildings, has changed greatly since Victorian times. The most common form of guttering used in Australia between 1870 and 1910 was of the pattern known as ogee (pronounced 'oh gee'). Half-round guttering was used before the appearance of the ogee pattern. Ogee guttering is still available today, although it has yet to make an appearance

at the neighbourhood hardware store. The cost is slightly higher than that of contemporary patterns in guttering but its use is recommended where authenticity is sought.

Checking the route by which stormwater is transported from the roof into the street is an unglamorous and uninteresting task which is often neglected. A good deal of damage can result, particularly in buildings in which the dampcourse is nearing the end of its life. Excessive ground moisture resulting from cracked or broken earthenware pipes in the drainage system can contribute to a variety of building faults and problems.

A drainage line can be tested quite simply by placing a hose in the downpipe at the point where it leaves the guttering. After the hose has been turned on water should begin to flow into the street from the outlet hole in the gutter at the front or rear of the house. If water does not appear within a minute or two the line is blocked and will have to be repaired or replaced. The first step in checking the nature of the problem is to take a long, firm object such as a stick, rod or length of thick wire and poke it into the pipe at the point where it discharges into the street. If the obstruction is close to the outlet and consists of an accumulation of mud, perhaps centred around some solid object, it may be possible to clear the line.

It will often be found that earthenware pipes passing under a footpath have been broken by local government employees or contractors working on resurfacing the path. Other blockages can occur as a result of cracking in old earthenware pipes due to movement of the ground or building or the activities of gardeners. Some minor blockages may be cleared by building up water pressure inside the pipe with the use of a hose and a makeshift seal formed from rag, wadded tightly around the hose.

Blockages occurring midway through a winding length of drainage line can be located by inserting a firm but pliable object such as a length of hosepipe. When the obstruction is reached the hose should be marked at the point where it enters the line and then withdrawn and laid on the ground above the pipeline to discover the approximate location of the blockage. It should be borne in mind that there may be more than one obstruction or fault in the length of an old drainage system. If the system is considered beyond repair it should be replaced with a new one consisting of P V C piping. The requirements of the local government authority should be ascertained before a footpath is opened to lay a new drainage line into the street.

The coating of stucco, commonly known today as render, protected Victorian houses from the entry of moisture. It should not be removed

Victorian builders marked grooves on external render to simulate the appearance of stone. Cleaning out the grooves prior to painting will bring back the appearance of the neat stone blocks and courses known as ashlar

WALLS: STUCCO AND PLASTER

STUCCO

The coating of render, or stucco as it was known, which was applied to the outside walls of Victorian and Edwardian houses served to protect and decorate the exterior of domestic buildings. It was usually marked or lined to give the appearance of the neatly formed and laid blocks of stone known as ashlar, although no real attempt was made to deceive. It was simply that this was a custom which had been part of British and hence colonial building practice for much of the nineteenth century and thus was not lightly discarded. The lines relieved the blank surface of the walls and provided a pleasing, regular pattern. A significant body of architectural thought in both Britain and Australia preferred what they considered to be the greater honesty and integrity of Georgian architecture with its reliance on exposed brickwork. The use of stucco was described as an 'abominable practice' of which 'too much cannot be said in severe condemnation'.[7] Where stucco was left unpainted for some reason it was ridiculed as 'elephant colour'.[8]

Despite the condemnation, there is no doubt that stucco served a very real purpose, especially in houses constructed in Australia before the introduction of cavity walls. The great majority of houses built prior to 1890 were constructed with solid walls of soft, porous sandstock brick. These were used before the widespread adoption of machine-pressed common bricks in the 1880s.

The apparent simplicity of early building methods conceals a greater sophistication and understanding of important principles than is commonly believed. A typical external wall on a Victorian building is composed of bricks, an internal layer of plaster coated with paint or wallpaper, and an external coating of render or stucco which again is coated with paint. These form a system which, if tampered with by the unwary, can result in serious problems from damp.

It has been common practice among inexperienced renovators in particular to strip the render from external walls and the plaster from internal walls of old houses. This not only destroys the original character of the buildings but opens the way for the destructive entry of water. Sandstock bricks in Victorian terraces were never meant to be seen. They were laid in haste in the safe knowledge that any defects in the bricklayers' work would be hidden beneath half an inch of render or plaster. A solid sandstock brick wall without the protection of stucco can soak up literally tonnes of water, each brick absorbing as much as half a litre. Much of this moisture will pass through the wall and, over a period of time, can cause considerable damage inside the house. Too soft and porous to be exposed to the atmosphere, sandstock bricks tend to decay and crumble if the protective render is removed. 'When the knowledge exists that the outside is to be covered . . . little attention is given to the facial appearance of the bricks and the method of laying them.'⁹

The complexity of the system formed by the apparently simple combination of brick, plaster and paint is illustrated by the fact that it will repel external moisture while retaining the characteristic of 'breathing' and allowing any moisture which does find its way into the wall to escape and evaporate safely. As the majority of Victorian buildings were constructed without the cavity between the two 'skins' of brick that is customary today, moisture could pass through a wall with comparative ease. It was therefore important that moisture in a wall, perhaps arising from the combined effects of weakness in the dampcourse and a period of heavy rain, should be able to travel to the surface and escape. Paints used both internally and externally were a working part of this complex system. They repelled water but were not impervious. Modern paints used on old houses should be of a type that permits this 'breathing' process to continue. Selection of an unsuitable paint may result in the formation of bubbles and eventual flaking as moisture tries to escape from the surface of the wall.

Houses at the corner of Brunswick and Gertrude Streets in the Melbourne suburb of Fitzroy, 1866

A variety of Victorian cornice profiles, Plate III from R S Burn's New Guide to Masonry, Bricklaying and Plastering

Plaster decoration on the entrance hall arch of a Victorian house in Glenferrie Road, Kew, Victoria

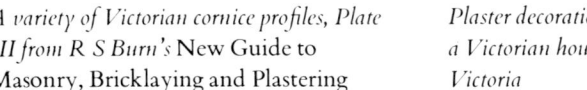

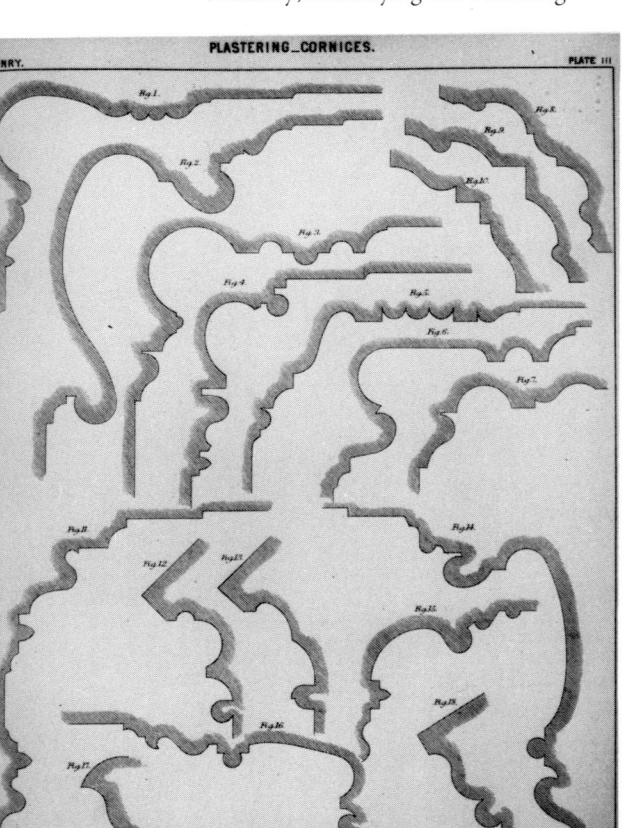

Care in the selection of paint applies also to the interior surfaces of walls. Retention and, if necessary, repair of the plaster surfaces inside the house is essential in rooms which are to be restored.

PLASTER

Plaster used on the walls and ceilings and for decoration in houses of the nineteenth and early twentieth centuries consisted of a mixture of slaked rock-lime and sand, with animal hair added to bond the whole together. Later, cements were used for the base coats. The trade has declined since 1900 and appears to be on the verge of extinction. Today there are few plasterers who have been trained to the standards and type of workmanship that was commonly seen during the Victorian period. Lime plaster as a finish has largely been replaced by cement render which offers neither the smoothness nor the fine detail that is possible with plaster.

Plaster surfaces and detail were easily damaged and will frequently require either repair or replacement during restoration work on an old building.

WALLS   A house which has been occupied by generations of people will often wear on its plaster walls the signs of their activities, of children's play, and of the work of a succession of removalists. Rising damp is often the cause of serious damage to plaster and it is pointless to replaster until the cause has been remedied and the wall is thoroughly dry.

Cracks and minor holes in plaster walls may be repaired quite simply. Fine cracks should be gently raked out with a sharp instrument and wetted before filling. The aperture must be wide enough to allow access for sufficient filler to obtain a proper bond to the two opposing surfaces. A commercial filler of the type available at every hardware

Adding decorative mouldings to an entrance hall arch during restoration

store is suitable. Cracks or holes should be overfilled and then fine sanded to a level surface when dry. Only a really smooth surface is going to give the appearance of a first-rate job if the wall is to be painted, so near enough is not good enough. While wallpaper will cover many imperfections, paint may accentuate them. It should at the same time be said that a perfect surface is not always attainable in a house which has had a long and turbulent life.

Areas of weakness in the bond between the plaster and the brick or stone from which the wall is built can be found by gently tapping the surface. A hollow or 'drummy' sound indicates a faulty bond. Unless the plaster at this point is clearly in danger of collapse it is quite possible that the wall may not need repairs for years. Movement induced by hand pressure in these areas, however, is a clear indication that prompt replacement of the plaster is necessary.

Where large areas of walls require replastering, the approach recommended by some architects requires the use of the traditional lime plaster, using a lime mortar with hair added to form the scratch and float coats, and finished with a setting coat made with lime putty and fine sand. An alternative method is the use of a two coat system known as render and set. The first coating applied consists of a render containing a very small amount of cement. This coat is intended to bring the work to a true and even surface before the finishing or set coat is applied. A typical mix consists of ten parts of sand, two parts of lime and one part of cement. If the mix contains more cement cracking is likely to occur. The finishing or setting coat may consist of equal parts of hydrated lime and gypsum plaster. A good tradesman will be able to obtain a hard, smooth surface with a two coat plaster system.

CEILINGS   Lath and plaster was used to form ceilings throughout the period covered by this book. Timber battens were nailed to the underside of the ceiling joists at regular

Decorative plaster in the entrance hall at
Havilah, *built at Mudgee, N S W, c. 1870*

*Pressed metal ceilings, cornices and wall
panels were popular for their durability and
fire resistance. The process, patented by
E H C Wunderlich in 1888, provided strong
competition for the plaster trade*

A Wunderlich advertisement from Zions'
Building Trades Pocket Directory,
1908–09

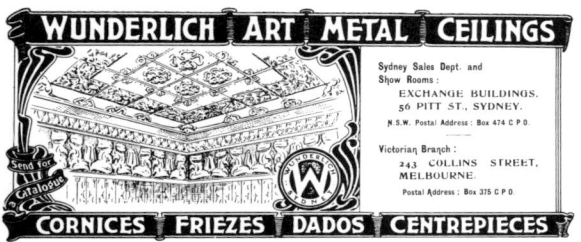

intervals across the room. The gaps between the laths usually approximated to the thickness of the workman's forefinger. Lime plaster, with animal hair worked into it, was
spread over the battens or laths and forced into the narrow gaps between them. The
knobs of plaster which formed between and above the laths created the bond or key
which held the ceiling in place. Over a long period of time deterioration can occur as
a result of rot in the laths or movement in the building, perhaps as a result of foot traffic
in upstairs rooms or thermal movement in the roof space. Water in even small quantities
can cause serious damage to a lath and plaster ceiling. The damage may not be apparent
for a long time but can result in rust weakening the nails which hold the laths to the
joists.

Sagging lath and plaster ceilings may often be repaired in cases where gravity appears
to be gaining the upper hand. If the trouble is caused by laths which have come loose
from the joists it may be possible to push the sagging area back into place, and screw or
nail the laths firmly against the joists. Clout-head nails or brass screws with large, flat
heads are used. This method requires knowledge of the location of the ceiling joists as
the screws or nails must enter solid timber to provide good, firm fixing. Screw or
nailheads should be slightly recessed into the surface and the resulting hollow filled with
plaster or filling compound. If sagging is the result of the loss of the bond between the
plaster and the laths a different method should be used. It may be possible to push the
plaster back hard against the laths and hold it there while fresh plaster is poured over
the top of the laths from above.

An alternative method which was used many years ago was to hold the loose plaster

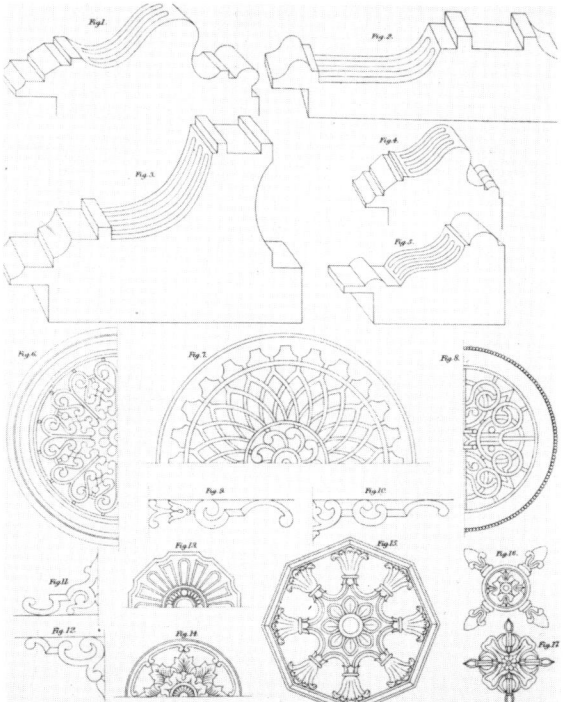

in place by fixing flat battens, about 60 mm wide, against the underside of the ceiling and nailing them firmly into the joists. The battens were set out in a regular pattern which appeared to be part of the ceiling decoration.

Where plaster has fallen from the ceiling, leaving areas of the laths exposed, it may be patched provided the laths are in good condition and are securely fastened to the joists. The replacement of an old ceiling may be carried out by fixing a new ceiling of plaster-board underneath it. The new ceiling should be held in place by screws or clout-head nails which are driven into the joists.

DECORATION   Original cornices and ceiling roses should be retained as far as possible. Most cornices were made on the job during the Victorian and Edwardian eras, 'run' in wet plaster by highly skilled tradesmen either on a workbench or against the ceiling. Damaged sections of original cornices may be repaired by the use of a template, prefer-ably cut from zinc or thin galvanised sheet, and prepared by drawing a cross section from part of the cornice which is in good repair.

Where an old cornice is missing or is beyond repair it should be replaced with a new cornice in the contemporary style, if not the precise shape, of the original. The replace-ment cornice will have been made in a fibrous plasterworks by the use of a mould. Its shape is therefore likely to differ from the original, and its profile is very likely to be less elaborate than that of its Victorian or Edwardian counterpart. An architect experienced in restoration work should be able to advise on the choice of a suitable manufactured cornice.

A typical Victorian plaster ceiling-rose. Pressed-metal roses were available in the Edwardian period

Plaster ceiling roses, reproduced to Victorian patterns, from the catalogue of the Melbourne firm of Picton Hopkins

Decorative Plaster Designs: Centre Panels and Wall Plaques

No. 170
1090 mm

No. 177
550 mm

No. 166
305 mm

No. 180
710 mm x
560 mm

No. 168
495 mm

No. 169
720 mm

Ceiling roses which have been seriously damaged can be replaced. A number of companies are making them today, often to patterns which were in use during the nineteenth century. Because the market for ceiling roses is smaller now than it was during Queen Victoria's day the range of sizes and styles is rather small in comparison. It will therefore not often be possible to obtain an identical match to the rose that is being replaced.

Replacing a ceiling rose can be an awkward and uncomfortable task. The services of an electrician may be required to remove and reconnect light fittings. The new rose should be smeared with plaster to help it adhere to the ceiling and either tied in position with wire looped over the ceiling joists, or firmly fixed with the aid of brass screws. Grooves cut by the wire in the surface of the rose, or the holes into which the screws have been worked, should be patched.

Some ceiling roses of modern manufacture may be too well made to be suitable for an old house. Victorian and Edwardian roses were made in rubber moulds and may display minor irregularities and imperfections. Modern fibreglass moulds produce perfect shapes.

A ceiling rose should always be selected with the scale of the room for which it is intended in mind. A large rose is not going to make a small room look imposing.

JOINERY

The staircases, doors, skirting boards and architraves of old houses are very seldom in original condition. Physical damage may consist of a variety of scars and scratches, thick layers of paint, or gaps cut into the timber to fit switches, locks or other items of modern hardware.

The action to be taken to make good this abuse must be governed by the degree of damage, its prominence after rooms have been furnished and occupied, and on the type of finish which will be used. Where the joinery is to be painted, stained, or grained it may be possible to repair it by filling with a commercial wood filler. Serious damage will require measures which may involve the replacement of affected timber with sections obtained from demolition sites, from stock in a joinery yard, or by arranging for a joinery to run new sections in the same timber and to the same pattern. The treatment required will vary in every case.

REPLACING SURFACE FINISHES

Any decision on action to be taken where the original joinery is still in reasonable condition and has not been painted should take into account the highly desirable patina of age. This is a quality of the surface that only time and perhaps the polishing of maids or previous owners can impart. The temptation to immediately begin stripping the old, darkened finish off mantelpieces, skirting boards, architraves and doors to reveal the bare surface of the timber should be resisted.

Folding panelled doors, often of cedar, were used to separate the dining room from the drawing room in Victorian houses

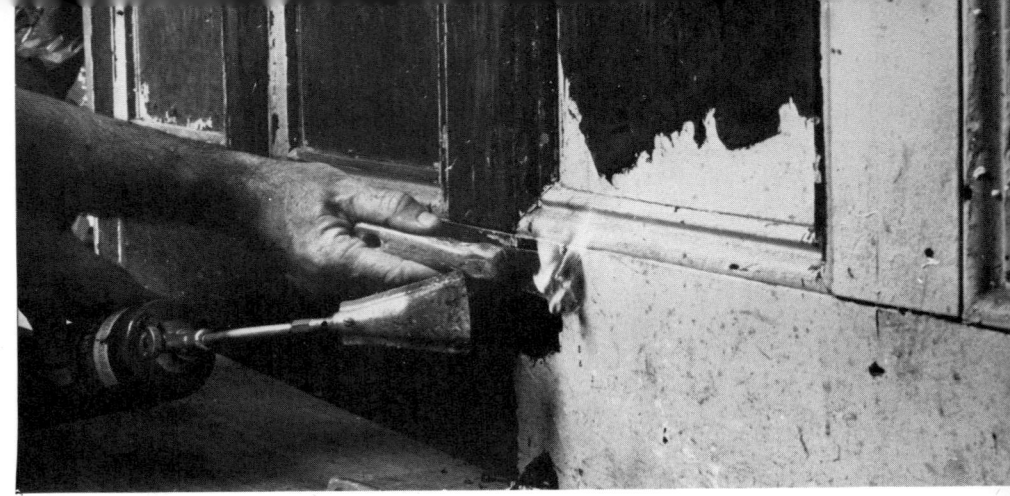

Design for front door; house at Neutral Bay for W T Angus, Esq., by Cyril Blacket, architect, Sydney

Careful cleaning with warm water and detergent or a commercial cleaning agent should be the first step. It may be found that this will give new life to an old surface and avert the need for a great deal of awkward, time-consuming and perhaps costly work. The patina of age is highly prized by dealers and collectors of old furniture and should be similarly appreciated as a quality of the joinery in old houses. Removal of the original finish is justified in those cases where it has become so darkened with age and deterioration that details are lost and the joinery appears black and unattractive. This is often the case with varnished timbers.

Builders of Victorian and Edwardian houses employed a variety of finishes on joinery work. It was commonly varnished, waxed, painted, marbled or grained. The original finish will often have been lost under layers of paint, applied so thickly that many fine details will have been obscured. Where joinery has been painted tests should be conducted at key points throughout the rooms to be restored in order to discover the original finish. Several points should be tested as the finish may vary from room to room and on different portions of the joinery within a room. Paint scrapings can be carried out by means of a razor blade, scalpel or sharp chisel.

A record of the finishes identified should be kept for reference purposes throughout the restoration programme. This may be in the form of a notebook with samples of the original finishes kept under clear plastic film and their locations marked on an accompanying plan of the rooms. Large samples will enable more accurate and easy colour matching and facilitate the restoration process. Always try to retain an area of the original finish, perhaps on a small section of skirting board or architrave, as an indication to future owners that an authentic restoration has been carried out.

In seeking the original finish it is worth noting that doors were rarely marbled although skirting boards and architraves were. A marble door would have been a practical impossibility and the Victorians, practised fakers though they were, invariably sought to emulate reality. (Further details on graining and marbling may be found on page 104.)

Removal of the joinery simplifies the task of cleaning, no matter what method is employed, but this is a job for the most skilled of owner/restorers or for a sympathetic and painstaking carpenter or joiner.

When removal of the original finish is considered necessary, the method used will depend on the type of finish, the shape and ornamentation of the joinery, the time available to the restorer and the type of replacement finish that is to be applied. Paint can be burnt off, scraped off either dry or with the aid of a commercial paint stripper, or removed by dipping the timber in a caustic bath. Caustic dipping, usually carried out by dealers in 'stripped' furniture, is not recommended for anything other than pine or joinery which is to be painted as it imparts a lifeless, unattractive appearance. Cedar is very badly affected by this process. Sandblasting is a fourth alternative but may take off not only the paint but also the shape of the mouldings which are an important part of the appeal of old joinery. Dry scraping can result in a scratched surface and damaged mouldings while

Typical timber decoration on the facade of a
Federation *house, Ashfield, N S W*

wet scraping, aided by the use of a paint stripper, is a messy business and one which may result in chemical burns to bare skin.

Painting tradesmen will usually burn off old paint before renewing the finish. The use of a large gas bottle with a long hose and a light, fan-shaped burner is recommended. Practice will result in the development of a deft touch which will avoid any scorching to the timber. The burner should be used in conjunction with a set of scrapers; flat, triangular and shaped. A couple of sharp chisels are also useful. Frequent sharpening with the aid of an oilstone is advisable. Skill is quickly developed and the process itself is swift and effective.

Varnish can be removed with a fine abrasive such as steel wool or sandpaper, or dissolved with methylated spirits. The resulting solution should be wiped off quickly with a clean rag.

Recreating the original finish may be a task for a highly skilled tradesman, particularly if graining or marbling is involved. Such people can be found but not always quickly or easily. The attainment of a high standard of authenticity and a superbly finished house often depends to a very large degree on the owner's determination and dedication. French polishing provides a hard, durable and transparent finish which preserves timber and highlights its beauty. It can be made from the following recipe: orange shellac, 350 g; benzoin, 30 g; sandarach, 30 g; methylated spirits, 2·25 l.

The surface of the timber should first be filled with plaster of Paris and methylated spirits. This should be allowed to dry and then sanded smooth. A piece of wadding is dipped into the polish and then covered with soft cloth to which a small quantity of linseed oil is applied. This is rubbed gently onto the timber in the direction of the grain, and then across the grain in a series of sweeping movements. This process is repeated until an acceptable finish is obtained. The polish should be allowed to dry for twelve hours, lightly sanded with fine paper, and another coat applied. The process may be repeated until a satisfactory appearance is obtained. The timber should then be rubbed with a clean cloth soaked in methylated spirits.

A warm and attractive appearance to cedar and other quality joinery timbers can be imparted by the application of a mixture of beeswax and mineral turps. The beeswax is melted in a saucepan or similar metal container and allowed to cool slightly. Sufficient turps should be added to form a waxy polish that is applied with a soft cloth. The timber should first be sealed with white French polish, available from the supplier listed in the 'Directory', page 130. The wax is used sparingly and any excess should be rubbed off. A clean cloth should be used to polish the surface to an attractive sheen. This simple process, used from early in the Australian colonial period, provides a very satisfactory and appealing finish. It is not suitable for use on pine.

Staircase at Havilah, Mudgee, N S W.
Brass rods and clips hold the carpet runner in place. Treads and risers on both sides of staircase carpeting were often painted with black japan

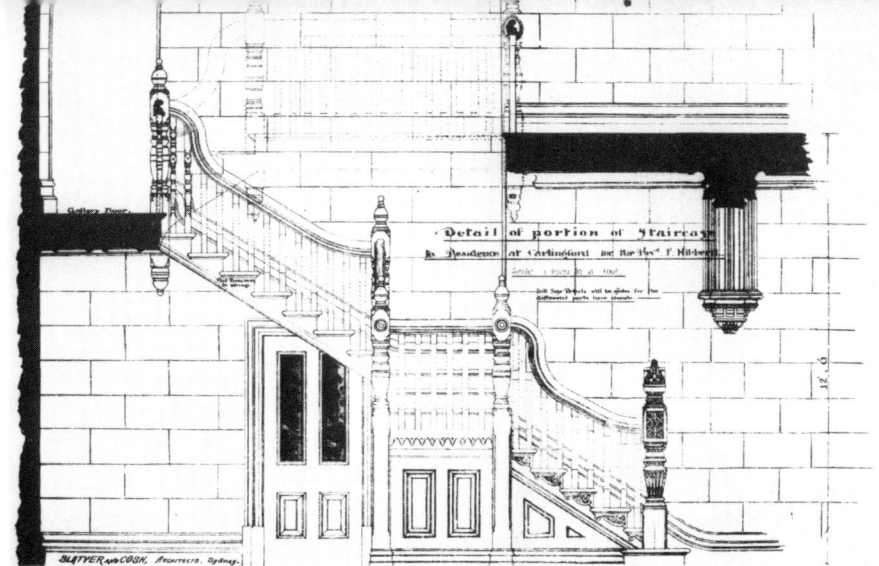

Detail of portion of staircase to residence at Carlingford N S W for the Reverend F Hibberd; from the Australasian Builder and Contractor's News, *17 June 1893*

Restoring the joinery in a badly abused house can be an arduous and uninteresting task but it is a vital part of any restoration programme and will pay ample dividends in terms of the rich, warm appearance of beautiful timber prepared and finished as the builders of the house intended it to be seen.

STAIRS

'Stair building is now founded upon fixed and unalterable principles. It is a distinct and separate branch of architecture, and is ranked among the most beautiful and useful of the arts.' The author of *The Carpenter and Joiner, Stair Builder and Handrailer*[10] was giving vent to justified pride in his trade. By 1870, when that book was published, the art of staircase building had reached heights which are unlikely to be attained again in a more utilitarian era.

Construction of staircases had been refined and developed for centuries in England and the craft came to Australia in the minds of the thousands of English, Scottish and Irish tradesmen who emigrated during Victoria's reign. Skilled carpenters and joiners took pride in their ability to create the stunning effects that richly carved and decorated staircases provided in the entrance halls of better quality houses. Elaborate newell posts, turned balusters and shaped handrails, often of cedar, that swept up to the privacy of the bedrooms contributed to the inviting appearance that the developers and builders of the era knew to be the requirements of their market. There is no doubt that a good staircase was an excellent selling point.

Each staircase was carefully graded in terms of quality and size of timber, carving and finish to suit the relative affluence of the prospective purchasers. The fact that so many buildings were part of a terrace group resulted in economies in materials and labour that often enabled such finishing details as staircases to be of better quality than might otherwise have been expected. Six or a dozen newell posts of one particular fancy design could be produced for a lower unit cost than one. Joiners who had to knock together twelve staircases developed individual and team skills that resulted in faster production with every one that was built. After reaching a peak in the closing years of the nineteenth century the art of staircase construction began to fall into a decline to which changing tastes, the 1890s depression and rising costs all made a contribution. They were, in the main, of a less ostentatious design after 1900.

The staircase that has survived almost unscathed the wear and tear of the generations and the onslaught of the painter's brush is a rare treasure and deserving of continued respectful treatment. Staircases that have been abused throughout the years and that are to be returned to their former beauty require careful attention.

Present-day faults in staircases are very rarely the fault of their builders who created beautiful objects that were both functional and highly durable. Probably the worst damage that will be found on an old staircase will be thick and badly applied coats of paint.

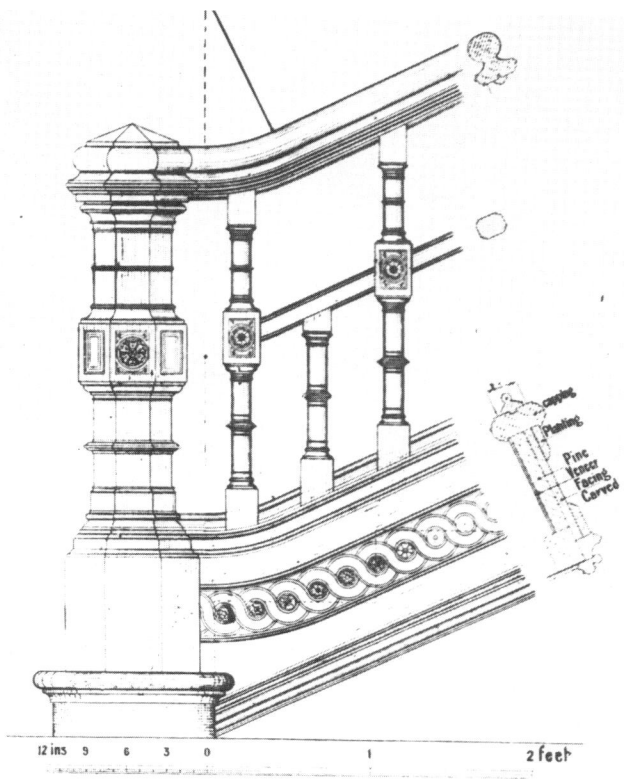

Part of a staircase, from W and A Mowatt's
A Treatise on Stairbuilding and
Handrailing, *1900*

The very large number of surfaces, often small and in confined areas, makes removal of paint a difficult and time-consuming operation. It should be noted that at least some parts of a staircase, if not all, may always have been painted.

Partial dismantling may expedite the process of removing excessive paint and preparing for the restoration of the original finish. Balusters were often of pine and can therefore be immersed in a caustic bath without damage. Cedar and other better quality timbers should not be dipped. Where dipping is not advisable or not possible commercial paint strippers may be useful although they can tend to cause traces of the paint to soak into the grain. The careful use of the gentle flame of a gas burner is probably the best available method of stripping paint from an old staircase.

Sharp chisels, scrapers, small rasps, sandpaper, steel wool and mineral turps will take off paint that the burner leaves behind. It is best not to use the burner on those parts of the staircase, such as the handrail, that are to be waxed. The large triangular panel, the spandrel, that fills in the side underneath many staircases can be removed without too much trouble and placed flat on trestles for greater convenience of access during paint removal. Wherever possible cleaning should be done *in situ* as dismantling may cause damage.

Repairs to the timber are usually best carried out by a sympathetic carpenter or joiner. Worn or damaged treads should be replaced or patched. Joinery yards can turn out replacements for missing balusters if they are supplied with one to copy.

Creaking staircases may be silenced by screwing the back of each tread into the riser. Ensure that the screws do not split the timber by selecting a suitable gauge and by partially drilling the holes for the screws. Treads may be stiffened by screwing battens to their underside, against the front riser.

DOORS

The characteristic panelled doors used throughout last century and into the twentieth century add interest and appeal to old houses. They should be replaced, if missing, or repaired wherever necessary.

The panelled front door of a late Victorian timber cottage, Neutral Bay, N S W

The entrance hall of a simple Victorian cottage. The two-toned architrave around the front door and large drawback rimlock are typical of the period

A panelled internal door with porcelain fingerplate and brass door furniture. A brass cabin hook holds the door open against the skirting board

Previous property owners who attempted to modernise old houses sometimes avoided the cost of fitting a new door by attaching two sheets of thin building board over both surfaces of the original door. The old rimlock, handles and fingerplates were discarded as they were out of character with the new, more modern appearance of the door which was then painted in a fashionable shade, usually cream, green or brown. The rest of the joinery invariably received a coat of the same paint.

The presence of an old door beneath what appears to be the smooth surface of a modern flush door can be detected by looking at the edge. The edge of the original door will be seen, sandwiched between its modern surfaces. The door will be a good deal heavier than a modern door. Its weight can be felt by swinging it from one hand to the other. Pushed, it will close with considerable impact. It may be restored by removing the sheets of building board, stripping the paint from its edges and any other surfaces, and replacing the original lock, handles and fingerplates with others in the same style. The shape and size of the lock and fingerplates can often be detected in the 'shadow' left on the door by the fading of its original finish, or by the addition of later finishes which were invariably applied over all door fittings. When these were removed for the application of the building board bare patches were left which conform to the outline of the original fittings.

Before beginning repairs to an old door the architrave on the inside of the room should be carefully examined. Changing tastes and fashions have resulted in many almost unnoticeable alterations being made to Victorian and Edwardian buildings. The Victorians in particular had a different concept of the role of interior doors. They were hung so that even when partially open they tended to obscure the view into the room. Doors 'should be hung so as to conceal the interior of the rooms as much as possible', wrote W B Tuthill in *The Suburban Cottage*,[11] published in 1885. In the more relaxed and open attitudes that developed during the twentieth century doors were frequently rehung on the other side of the frame so that the contents of the room were revealed as soon as the door was opened. Gaps in the frame and architrave will often indicate the original positions of the hinges and lock staple of a door that has been re-hung. It may be found that efforts have been made to fill these gaps, with varying degrees of success. Doors should be replaced in their original position in order to revive that part of the atmosphere and feeling of privacy which they contributed to the house when it was first built.

Missing or damaged mouldings to the panels should be replaced by others of the same size and style. These may be available from stock at large, specialist timberyards or joineries. Where no suitable replacement is available it should be possible to find a joinery which is willing to run new mouldings in the same pattern. If the door is to be painted virtually any light timber will suffice but clear or light finishes may require the use of the same or a very similar timber, or special attention to ensure that the new moulding is stained to match the older existing mouldings. When new mouldings are to be specially cut, the total quantity that will be required throughout the building should be ascertained and ordered all at once.

Doors that have been fitted with unsuitable locks of a later period or otherwise damaged will require repairs which are usually best made by a skilled carpenter or joiner. Timber blocks can be cut and fitted into gaps or damaged areas in a way that will barely be noticed once the redecoration has been completed. Filling gaps or cracks is facilitated if the door is to be painted. Repairs may be more noticeable with other finishes. Doors that are beyond repair should be replaced from the large stock usually available at demolition yards or demolition sites. Care should be taken not only with the size of the door but also to ensure that the size and number of the panels is the same as other doors in the building and that the replacement door has the same mouldings.

WINDOWS

By far the most common type of window used in Victorian and Edwardian houses was the double-hung sash window. Its simplicity and efficiency ousted its rivals from the vast majority of Australian houses during the period of its greatest popularity. It presents no particular problem for the restorer who will find that parts can be replaced and repairs can be made comparatively simply. The principal requirement will be time as windows in a building which has not been properly maintained will require some effort to bring them back into good working order. It will probably be necessary to remove both sashes from the frame during restoration work. It is advisable to provide an alternative means of closing the gap against weather and intruders as it may not be possible to make the repairs and replace the sashes on the same day. The length of time involved will depend on the state of the individual window.

Before starting work on a window it is advisable to check whether the frame is securely fixed to the surrounding brickwork, or timber in the case of a weatherboard house. The problem is most common in brick houses and occurs because of a deficiency in the manner in which the window was originally fixed. Different expansion and contraction rates of brick and timber, movement in the wall and the effects of weathering are the principal causes of loose window frames. Movement is often indicated by a gap between the brickwork or render and the frame. This can be seen on the outside of the building and has often been patched or filled with putty, cement, timber strips or other filling materials. All such material should be removed until the line of the original brickwork or render is seen. The size of the gap will then clearly indicate the extent of the movement that has occurred. All loose material in the gap should be raked out and the window frame gently but firmly tapped back to its original position or as far as it will go.

Care should be taken not to damage the frame, architrave, sash or the glass. The window should be securely fixed into position by drilling through the frame at the top and into the brickwork. A plastic plug can be inserted into the hole in the brickwork and the window screwed firmly into place. The holes in the frame may be filled with a suitable wood filler and repainted. If any gap remains on the outside of the window it should

A double-hung sash window on a Victorian cottage. The lace curtain on the lower sash, held in place by two rods attached by four brass clips, was a common feature in Victorian and Edwardian houses

be filled with a commercial filler suitable for exterior use between masonry and timber.

In repairing windows rotten or damaged timber will frequently be encountered. Each problem has to be assessed in the light of the extent of the deterioration and the possibility of satisfactory repairs being made without major trouble and expense. Hardwood sills which have not been painted for some years will frequently crack and split but may often be repaired when apparently beyond salvation. Very dry sills should first be primed, then filled with putty to which extra linseed oil has been added. Commercial fillers may be used, provided they are suitable for use on exterior woodwork. After the sills have been repaired the undercoat and one or two finishing coats of paint are applied. Stocks of hardwood sills are still held by some of the older timberyards should replacement be necessary.

The brickwork or render should be examined where it meets the sill on the outside of the building if there is evidence of moisture on the wall inside the house. The bricks or render should slip neatly underneath the sill, thus ensuring that rainwater runs off and does not find its way into the house. Cracks or gaps in render, stone or brickwork, or sills that fail to shed water efficiently, can result in dampness inside the house. Dampness arising from this cause can normally be distinguished from rising damp as it will usually be found immediately under or to the side of the window. Redecoration in such circumstances is a waste of time until the cause of the problem has been found and rectified.

Broken sashcords are common. Sashes must be removed to fit new cord which is available from hardware stores. On each side of the window frame, at the bottom of the groove or track in which the sash slides, a small timber panel can be lifted out to retrieve the cast iron weight which will be found at the bottom of the space behind the panel. Missing or irretrievable weights must be replaced by others of the same size. The size of the weight depends on the size and weight of the sash. Sash weights were the most common cast-iron objects found in early houses and can be obtained from demolition sites and demolition contractors.

The thin strips of timber which separate one sash from the other are known as parting moulds or beads. One of these may be damaged while taking out the sashes. Suitable replacements can be obtained from timber yards. One parting mould per window was intended to be removable when the window was originally made and fitted in order to facilitate sash cord replacements. However, the temptation for later owners to firmly nail and paint it into place has usually been irresistible, and its removal without splitting or breaking has thus been made virtually impossible. Its replacement may be fixed in position with two light nails to facilitate future repairs.

Removal of the sashes provides an excellent opportunity to clean excess and accumulated paint from the frame and thus ensure that both sashes will slide easily and smoothly when replaced. This is also the time to repaint sashes and frames.

Replacing broken or cracked panes of glass is a task that is best left to a glazier. It may be more economical and convenient to take the sashes to the glazier while the window is dismantled for repair than to have a house call made. Perfectionists may choose to ignore minor cracks or damage to original panes of glass in the belief that its characteristic 'ripple' effect is part of the character of a building which dates from an age when the quality of glass was not as high as it is today. If old glass must be replaced it may be necessary to fit larger sash weights. Lead strips wound around the sash cord at the top of the sash weights will also provide the extra weight required to balance the heavier, modern glass.

Glazing bars are a relic of an era when it was not possible to produce the large panes of sheet glass which are available today. The number of glazing bars per window was gradually reduced as glass-making technology improved. However, they were still common in windows produced late in the nineteenth century as their use reduced the cost of replacing broken panes. Glazing bars were frequently hacked out and larger panes fitted as the cost of glass began to fall in the first half of the twentieth century. The original presence of glazing bars can usually be detected by marks on the sash frame. They should be replaced.

Victorian and Edwardian windows were furnished with a wide range of hardware, usually of brass or bronze. Security was provided by means of a sash fastener of brass, often topped with a porcelain knob. Although later models were improved to foil burglars, this type of catch fell into disuse and was often replaced after it was found that a knife slipped between the sashes could be used to disengage the catch. The lower sash was equipped with a brass sash lift which conveniently opened the window when a finger was hooked beneath it. An alternative type with a loop or circle of brass into which a finger was slipped to open the window was known as a sash eye. The lower sash often boasted four curtain clips designed to hold the horizontal rods on which curtains of lace or other materials were fitted. These clips were quickly snapped open to allow the curtain to be removed for washing.

Sash fasteners and lifts came in a great variety of styles. Most old houses, even those which have been badly abused, will contain several original sash fasteners and lifts. Bedrooms and lesser rooms may provide sufficient original fittings to furnish windows in the dining and sitting rooms. Where original sash fasteners cannot be replaced modern brass reproductions of old-fashioned styles are available from specialist retailers of quality architectural hardware. Brass founders can make new castings of small, simple items such as sash lifts provided a sample is available. Attention to such detail as this is the mark of the meticulous restorer.

SHUTTERS

Shutters provided protection from the light and the heat of the sun, rain, prying eyes and intruders. Their usefulness is particularly apparent in houses which are exposed to the direct heat of the afternoon sun in summer. Closing the shutters will assist in reducing the temperature in the house to a far more comfortable level. The use of shutters also permits windows to be opened in circumstances when rain would normally enter the house.

Restoration of nineteenth-century houses will frequently involve the replacement or repair of shutters. Many thousands of shutters were removed from houses in inner urban areas of our larger cities during the first half of the twentieth century. Whether adding or taking away, almost every building activity leaves marks on a house and it is usually fairly simple to discover if shutters were originally fitted.

Evidence of the original presence of shutters on an old house will usually consist of gaps where the hinges were fitted to the window frames and the flaps that once held the shutters open against the walls. The flaps may have been removed but can usually be detected by the presence of small patches in the mortar or render. In restoration, shutters should only be replaced on those windows or doors which are known to have been fitted with shutters. It was usual in many two-storeyed buildings to fit shutters only to windows and French doors on the ground floor. This was common practice in situations where the front of the house was sheltered from the heat of the sun. Shutters were fitted on the ground floor in such cases to provide security and privacy.

Replacement shutters may be obtained from demolition sites or dealers in old building materials. New shutters which are available from many timber dealers are usually too flimsy for restoration work but where funds are limited they may be better than nothing. Suitable shutters can be obtained from joineries but are far more expensive as they are normally made to order. A higher cost can be expected where shutters must be made to fit round-headed windows.

Parliament hinges and shutter flaps on a window on which the shutters have been restored

Dining room fireplace, Coombing Cottage, Carcoar, N S W

Uniformity of design and finish reinforces the architectural effect of terraced housing, creating a pleasing streetscape; Glebe, N S W

Shutters fixed to Victorian houses were normally made of cedar, Baltic pine or Californian redwood. They consisted of two leaves, each composed of a light frame filled in with louvres set on a slant. Window shutters contained a top, middle and bottom rail while those for French doors were normally more substantially constructed with a wide centre rail.

In ordering shutters from a joinery detailed drawings with all dimensions will normally be required, except where a sample shutter is supplied. The width and height can be deduced from the apertures to be filled while the dimensions of the timber to be used may be taken from old shutters of comparable size. Detail such as the beading which was normally run on each edge of the stile or frame in order to provide a grip for fingers is important if authenticity is to be obtained.

Shutters should always be painted in a house that is being restored to its Victorian appearance. Painting shutters is a job that is best done before they are fitted. They are hung on Parliament hinges which enable them to open back against the outer face of the wall.

FIREPLACES

In our homes—those shrines of our dearest affections—if there is one place more hallowed than another, it must surely be the fireplace round which all our domestic associations seem to centre—that spot which is ever bright in our memory, with the recollection of happy hours, and of the purest and tenderest emotions we have known . . . .[12]

From Sands' Sydney Directory, *1861*

Despite the great affection which it had aroused in Victorian and Edwardian times, the open fire in its cast-iron register grate, tucked beneath a timber or marble mantel which was often elaborately carved, was a frequent casualty of the long, dark age in which many of the inner suburbs of Australian cities were regarded as slums.

Its fall from fashion can be attributed to a number of factors including the introduction of electricity and the consequent development of efficient and economical electric heaters, the gradual phasing out of domestic servants, the end of regular deliveries by vendors of coke and coal, and to changing social attitudes. Fires could be a nuisance to light, filling the house with smoke and dirtying the paint, furnishings and curtains. A grate full of ash had to be cleaned up a long time after the pleasures of the fire had been forgotten. In smaller houses the dry storage of fuel was often another source of nuisance. The inconvenience and expense of the daily use of open fires was recognised in the nineteenth century when no real alternative existed.

Many efforts were made to improve their design and alleviate some of the problems associated with their use. In 1855, Dr Neil Arnott published a book entitled *On the Smokeless Fireplace: Chimney Valves and other means of obtaining healthy warmth and ventilation.* Although there is little evidence that Dr Arnott's chimney valves found much favour with builders or architects, his book provides an insight into the feelings which resulted in so many fireplaces being ripped out in the twentieth century.

During the time every morning while the fires are being lighted, the rooms cannot be used; and there is, besides, much annoyance from smells, smoke, dust and noise. When neglect of servants lets the fire go out in the course of the day, it has to be lighted again.

One of several elaborate fireplaces in
Kerribree, Hereford Street, Glebe, N S W.
The house was built in 1889

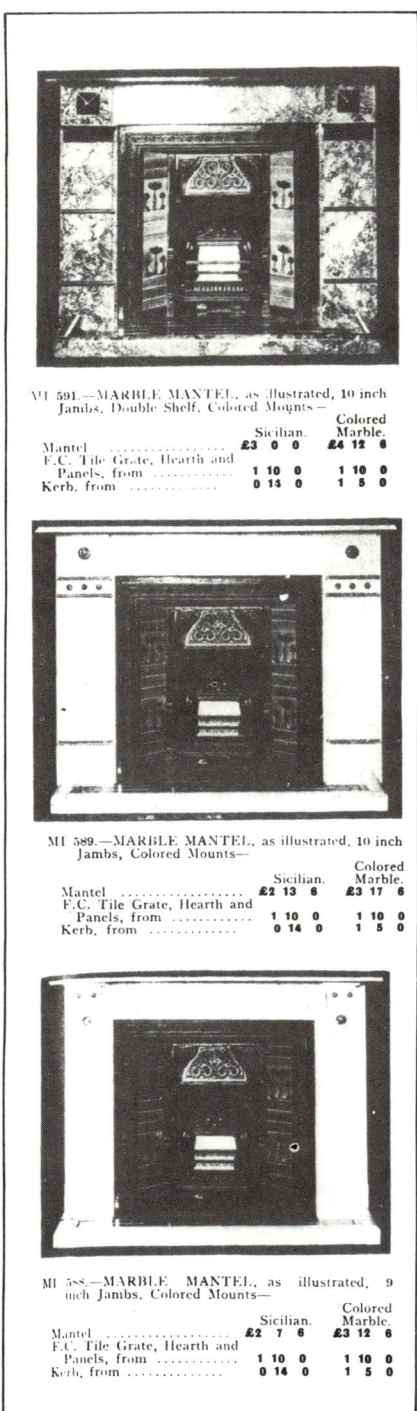

MI 591.—MARBLE MANTEL, as illustrated, 10 inch
Jambs, Double Shelf, Colored Mounts—

	Sicilian.	Colored Marble.
Mantel	£3 0 0	£4 12 6
F.C. Tile Grate, Hearth and Panels, from	1 10 0	1 10 0
Kerb, from	0 14 0	1 5 0

MI 589.—MARBLE MANTEL, as illustrated, 10 inch
Jambs, Colored Mounts—

	Sicilian.	Colored Marble.
Mantel	£2 13 6	£3 17 6
F.C. Tile Grate, Hearth and Panels, from	1 10 0	1 10 0
Kerb, from	0 14 0	1 5 0

MI 588.—MARBLE MANTEL, as illustrated, 9
inch Jambs, Colored Mounts—

	Sicilian.	Colored Marble.
Mantel	£2 7 6	£3 12 6
F.C. Tile Grate, Hearth and Panels, from	1 10 0	1 10 0
Kerb, from	0 14 0	1 5 0

*Marble mantelpieces and their prices, from the
1909 catalogue of the Sydney merchants
F Lassetter and Company*

To light the fire in the morning, and to keep it alight with tolerable uniformity during the day, the frequent attendance and labour of a servant is required—much increasing the expense of the fire.[13]

As the trend away from open fires became evident, the number of recruits to the trade of chimney sweep began to diminish, although a few still survive today in our larger cities. Open fires are not likely to achieve again the role in home heating which they held in earlier decades, but there is no doubt that their popularity is higher than for many years. Today, they are mainly used to supplement other forms of heating and to provide the special atmosphere that an open fire adds to home life or social gatherings. The fireplace, whether in use or not, is the focal point of any room.

Where fireplaces have been removed from an old house they can often be readily replaced, particularly where the brickwork of the chimney and chimney breast is intact. Where this has been demolished the re-instatement of the fireplace is a more expensive and difficult procedure, calling for the services of a bricklayer experienced in the unusual and difficult art of building a fireplace that won't fill the house with smoke. The necessary skills are more likely to be found among bricklayers from the U K. The Commonwealth Experimental Building Station's pamphlet, *Notes on the Science of Building: Fireplaces*, is a useful publication. It is available from offices of the Department of Housing and Construction or from the Australian Government Publishing Service.

MANTELPIECES

The mantelpieces or chimneypieces are one of the principal decorative elements in the dining room and drawing room of an old house. Their name is an indication of their role: using 'piece' in the artistic sense to denote a specimen of handicraft or a work of art. As such, their replacement or repair warrants considerable thought and attention to detail.

This extraordinary fireplace with inglenook was photographed in a house in Perth c. 1905

MI 565.—WOOD MANTEL, as illustrated, Stained or Enamelled, with Imitation Marble Panels—
Mantel 22 6
F.C. Grate, Print Hearth .... 20 -
If Mantel square opening, 2/6 less.

MI 564.—WOOD MANTEL, as illustrated, Stained or Enamelled, with Imitation Marble Panels—
Mantel 22 6
F.C. Grate, Print Hearth 20,-
Cast Iron Kerb as shown, 17/6
If Mantel square opening, 2/6 less.

MI 587.—WOOD MANTEL, as illustrated, Stained
Mantel 17 6
F.C. Grate, Print Hearth .... 20 -
Marble Kerb from 12/6
If Mantel Primed, 2/6 less.

Inexpensive timber mantelpieces were often made to resemble marble or grained to resemble more expensive timbers such as walnut, rosewood, oak or cedar

Despite the allusions to artistry inherent in the name, mantelpieces were stock lines in the warehouses and stores of merchants who specialised in building materials. They could be ordered off the floor by architects and builders and were available in quantity if needed to complete the fitting out of a row of terraces. In Melbourne in the early 1890s the firm of Messrs Train, Weston and Robinson in Flinders Street was one of the larger suppliers: 'The marble mantelpieces are what principally arrest the eye. They are there in large numbers and in great variety, from the plain and inexpensive descriptions suitable for the best room of a workman's cottage to the ornate and costly designs for the mansions of the Toorak plutocracy.'[14]

Marble mantelpieces were generally preferred then, as they are today, for marble was justifiably regarded as being more elegant than timber or the rare alternative, cast iron. But there were always critics such as the one who told builders in 1890 that 'We do not want a structure of heavy mortuary marble, with a shelf to hold a lot of useless knick-nacks'.[15]

Marble is limestone in crystalline form and is generally found in the vicinity of igneous rock. When cut and polished it provides a superb glossy finish that has imparted prestige to homes and public buildings for thousands of years. Most marble mantels were imported as, although marble had been found in New South Wales, Queensland, South Australia and Victoria, the local quarries were not developed to the stage where easy, economical exploitation was possible. One exception was the quarry at Marulan near Sydney which supplied the marble for many a distinctive mantelpiece. The *Australasian Builders' and Contractors' Price Book* reported in 1891 that 'Marulan marble has for the last twenty years been made into very handsome mantelpieces, and is well known in Sydney'.[16]

Where economy dictated the use of timber for the mantels of a house, it was invariably painted to resemble marble, or grained to take on the appearance of more ex-

'For the comfort of a house a good grate is very necessary' wrote the author of Lassetter's 1909 catalogue. Cast-iron register grates were then available at prices ranging from 9/6 to 25/- for elaborate models with tiled side panels. Blac-it or Zebo may be used to provide an authentic finish to old grates

pensive woods. Timber mantels were in great demand. In Sydney, the Kauri Timber Company imported 500 mantels from New Zealand in 1891. New Zealand-made mantels were highly regarded in the building industry and '. . . for excellent pieces of the joiner's art are generally pronounced by the trade to be unequalled by similar work from any other part of the world'.[17]

At nearby Pyrmont, the firm of Saxton and Binns carried a large range of 'enamelled art mantels' at prices which ranged from 6/6 to 24/6. Stock sizes to suit 36 inch grates were available in various finishes including walnut, gold and marbled timber.[18] In better quality houses towards the end of the Victorian era timber mantelpieces were provided with elaborate overmantels, decorated with mirrors and turned and carved wood which added an ostentatious air. Mantelpieces in upstairs rooms were often of the same material as those in the dining and drawing room, but were normally carved and finished to a lower standard.

Quite strict rules on the selection and placement of colours and styles normally applied to marble mantelpieces. In the drawing room the mantelpiece was of white or grey marble to complement the light and feminine atmosphere of this room. It was also more highly decorated and carved than its dining room counterpart. The masculinity of the dining room was emphasised by its mantelpiece in black or the darker shades of grey, green or red. Exceptions to these rules of taste can certainly be found but they are unusual—a grey or soft pink marble mantelpiece may be found in a dining room, for example. If there are good reasons for believing it to be original the reason will probably lie in a scarcity of dark marble mantelpieces at the time of construction, or strong personal views on the part of the original builder or owners.

Such idiosyncracies should not be regarded as setting a precedent to be followed by present-day restorers. The rules on the placement of mantelpieces can serve as useful clues to the original purpose of rooms in an old house.

A marble mantelpiece of the Victorian or Edwardian period that does not require careful cleaning and polishing is a rare item. Even those with surfaces that are superficially quite satisfactory will often take on a new appearance when cleaned and polished. The process can be performed by members of the small but thriving group of craftsmen in marble who are still active in most of the larger cities of Australia.

Professional polishing, though often very expensive, will restore life that has been obliterated from the surface of the marble by the smoke and grime of generations. The work is usually performed in the workshop, rarely *in situ*. Where a secondhand mantelpiece has been purchased the awkward and potentially dangerous task of moving such a valuable and very breakable item can be minimised by immediately taking it to the workshop of a selected marble craftsman. A quote should be obtained before the mantelpiece is moved into the workshop. Prior telephone contact will eliminate marble merchants who are either not interested or are too expensive.

Where the cost of professional cleaning is too high or an owner wishes to avoid the cost and inconvenience of removing an existing mantelpiece, it can be cleaned *in situ* with results that are usually quite satisfactory. A specialty product for the cleaning of marble is available under the brand name of Vermarco. (The supplier's name and address is listed in the Directory, page 129.) Four tablespoons, i.e. 80 ml, of the cleaner is completely dissolved in 4·5 l of water. The solution should be liberally applied to the surface by sponge, cloth, mop, brush or roller. For best results, it should be spread over only as much surface as can be cleaned before drying takes place. The solution should be allowed to work on the surface for a minimum of five minutes before being cleaned off. The operation may be repeated if necessary. A slightly stronger solution consisting of seven tablespoons—150 ml—to the same quantity of water can be used for cleaning floors. Ver-

marco cleaner may also be used on slate, ceramic and stone.

A marble polish, Rigoli Bianca Rapida, is available from the same supplier. This should be applied very sparingly with a soft rag to a small area of the marble, no greater than 600 × 600 mm. It should be vigorously rubbed off immediately after application with a clean soft rag, generating as much friction heat in the process as possible. The application of more than the bare minimum of the polish will cause blotchy deposits to accumulate on the surface of the marble. These should be removed with a razor blade or scraper. Marble may also be cleaned with spirits of sorrell, rubbed in with hessian, and polished with putty powder. Spirits of sorrell and putty powder may be obtained from suppliers of industrial chemicals.

Damaged marble mantelpieces can often be successfully repaired by a marble craftsman. Parts which in their damaged state are a serious impairment to the beauty of the object can be mended or replaced.

Fitting a marble mantelpiece into position is a task for the sure of hand and confident. It was, traditionally, the job of the plasterer. Plaster of Paris or casting plaster was used to bond the parts of the mantelpiece together and, in conjunction with steel pins, to hold it firmly in position against the chimneybreast. Trading in mantelpieces is common in the larger cities where they are regularly advertised for sale, usually described as 'fireplaces'.

CHIMNEYS

Heat without smoke is the objective of the fuel combustion system incorporated in most of the houses built in Australia prior to World War I. The achievement of this objective is made possible by the deceptively simple but technically quite complex combination of grate, flue, chimney stack and chimney pot. Even today, many years after the end of the heyday of the open fire, many of the subtleties of this system are still not fully understood. There remains a degree of mystery about the technology of Victorian and Edwardian fireplaces which modern research has still not quite resolved. Opinions differ as to the desirable size and shape of the flue and the most effective method of ensuring that the smoke goes up the chimney and the heat stays in the room.

As chimneys were often removed during alterations to old houses it is important to understand, as far as possible, the principles that govern their operation. Chimneys were frequently demolished during re-roofing in order to avoid the cost and trouble associated with repairing or renewing the lead flashing, and with fitting the new roof around the chimney. It was usually a simple matter to knock off the brickwork to below roof level and carry the new roof over the hidden stump. People who did not light fires had no need of chimneys.

Fireside accessories, from the 1909 catalogue of F Lassetter and Company

A group of terraces with original chimney pots, still in place after 95 years; Boyce Street, Glebe, N S W

An old house without at least its major chimneys is a sorry sight. Its restoration will always be incomplete until they have been replaced. Rebuilding a chimney is a comparatively simple matter for a skilled bricklayer in those cases where the stump has been retained. However, working at a height may necessitate the use of scaffolding. Depending on the circumstances, keeping the bricklayer supplied with mortar and bricks can be an awkward task. Restoring a chimney becomes a far more complex and expensive operation when not only the chimney, but the chimney breast and all associated brickwork has been removed from inside the building. A careful examination is suggested before rebuilding is commenced in order to ensure that the system is being built in the right place and that an efficient, working fireplace will result. The advice of an architect experienced in restoration may be advisable.

The architects and builders of old Australian houses very largely followed the British practice of building the brickwork of the chimney and chimney breast on the inside of the wall, not as an attachment to the outside of the building. Thus, with most of the structure inside the house warmth escaping through the brickwork was retained. A good coat of plaster on the face and sides of the chimney breast prevented smoke from leaking into the room through crevices in the brickwork. The practice was obviously essential in the construction of terrace houses, while farmhouses and timber cottages were frequent exceptions to the rule.

When a chimney is being rebuilt, a hole is cut through the roof and the new brickwork is carried through to the height of the original structure. This is often easy to determine by comparison with chimneys in neighbouring houses, particularly when dealing with terraces. The chimney should be high enough to ensure that adjacent buildings will not tower over it and perhaps produce a pressure buildup that will force smoke back down into the house. It is now considered that the vertical height of a flue, including the chimney pot, should not be less than 4·6 m. A good updraught is essential to the efficient functioning of a chimney. Where no old chimneys are available to provide a comparison the following recommendations give a guide to the height to which the new chimney should be taken above the roof:

Chimney rises through the ridge	600 mm above the ridge
Chimney rises through the roof slope	750 mm above the ridge
Chimney rises through a flat roof	900 mm above the roof

The chimney of a Victorian house in the Italianate style, 1885

A minor masterpiece in brick and decorative cement; Glenferrie Road, Kew, Victoria

A plumber or reliable roofing contractor can be engaged to fit the flashing, usually strips of lead or aluminium, which prevents rainwater leaks from occurring where the chimney joins the roof. Modern chimneys are fitted with a tray, normally of sheet copper with a hole for the flue, which is built into the brickwork above the roof to prevent moisture working its way down into the house by soaking through the bricks. It need hardly be said that a new chimney should have the shape and appearance of an old chimney.

THE FLUE

The flue has an important bearing on the effectiveness of any chimney, although this is an area on which opinions differ, principally about its size and shape. Centuries after the first clumsy fuel combustion systems became a part of domestic architecture in England, innovative minds began to look for methods by which the efficiency of the ordinary home fire could be increased. Reference is made to 'the new chimney' in *A Treatise on Preventing Fires Smoaking* which was published in England in 1715. The definitive work was Count Rumford's essay, entitled *Of Chimney Fireplaces, and the principles of Chimney-construction*, which appeared in 1796. Rumford's recommendations were as follows:

○ A sloped fire-back;
○ A streamlined lintel to lead the room air into the flue without hindrance;
○ A deep, narrow throat, centrally placed above the grate. The throat to be 100 mm (4 in) wide and from 150 to 200 mm (6 to 8 in) deep with a rounded entrance ;
○ A flat smoke-shelf, level with the top of the throat, to stop soot and rain;
○ A small smoke-chamber;
○ Splayed sides and a definite narrowing of the fireplace towards the back. The flue to run from the smoke chamber to the top of the chimney in as straight a fashion as possible with any unavoidable bends being gentle and smooth.[19]

Rumford believed that kinks in the flue resulted in lower efficiency and contributed to the problem of smoke in the room. Bends in the flue were usually necessary in two-storeyed or higher houses, as fireplaces were normally located one above the other. The flues of the lower fireplaces had to be turned to one side or the other to avoid upstairs fireplaces. Later authorities came to believe that this bend in the flue, a result of necessity

The height of a chimney above the ridge of the roof and the influence of adjacent structures have an important bearing on its effectiveness

The range of chimney pots produced up until the 1960s by the Sydney firm of Fred A Mashman Pty Ltd. Pots number 6 and 7, as well as another which is not illustrated, are still part of their normal production. Numbers 2, 3 and 9 can be made if required

No. 1
Height 11 inches

No. 5
Height 12 inches

No. 7
Height 19 inches

No. 9
Loose Hood
Height 8 ins.

No. 10
Loose Hood
Height 9 ins.

No. 3
Height 16 inches

No. 2
Height 11 inches
C. Pot only

No. 4
Height 12 inches
C. Pot only

No. 6.
Height 24 inches

No. 8
Height 19 inches

Baffle C. Pot
Height 16 inches

in multi-storeyed houses, was a major factor in the creation of a successful chimney. *The Practical Brick and Tile Book*, published in 1886 and available in Australia the following year, suggested that the flue should measure 230 × 355 mm (9 × 14 in) and recommended: '. . . in building the flues, turn them first one way and then the other, so as to prevent the rain from falling down the chimney and also to give it a sharper draught.'[20]

Count Rumford's theories on the construction of fireplaces and chimneys are generally adopted today although recent research by Professor Rosin has resulted in some modifications that are now widely accepted in the construction of modern fireplaces in Britain. Whereas the size of the flue constructed in traditional nineteenth and early twentieth century buildings is normally 230 mm (9 in) square , Rosin has suggested a flue 300 mm (12 in) square .

CHIMNEY POTS AND COWLS

Chimney pots appear to have originated in seventeenth century France as a means of simplifying the construction of chimneys. Prior to their development, chimneys were often built in the form of a column or pedestal, with a cap formed in brick serving both an aesthetic purpose and to keep out rain and snow. The chimney pot produced the same result and by simplifying the task of the bricklayer resulted in reduced construction costs. It was invariably made of earthenware and required only a sound base upon which it was firmly fixed with mortar.

The large-scale use of chimney pots in Britain followed the English translation of M Gauger's *Fires Improved* in 1715. They aroused astonishing opposition from some British traditionalists. In a paper on the construction of chimneys, delivered to the International Health Exhibition in London in 1884, John P Seddon referred to chimney pots and cowls as 'fantastic creations', and as 'costly and ugly excrescences'. He believed cowls to be 'miserable metal makeshifts . . . [created] by the chimney-quacks'.

In Britain and Australia, Victoria's reign was the golden age of chimney pots. They were produced in a vast range of sizes, shapes, patterns and designs. The 1964 catalogue

A lobster-backed chimney cowl — a rare survivor from the 1880s

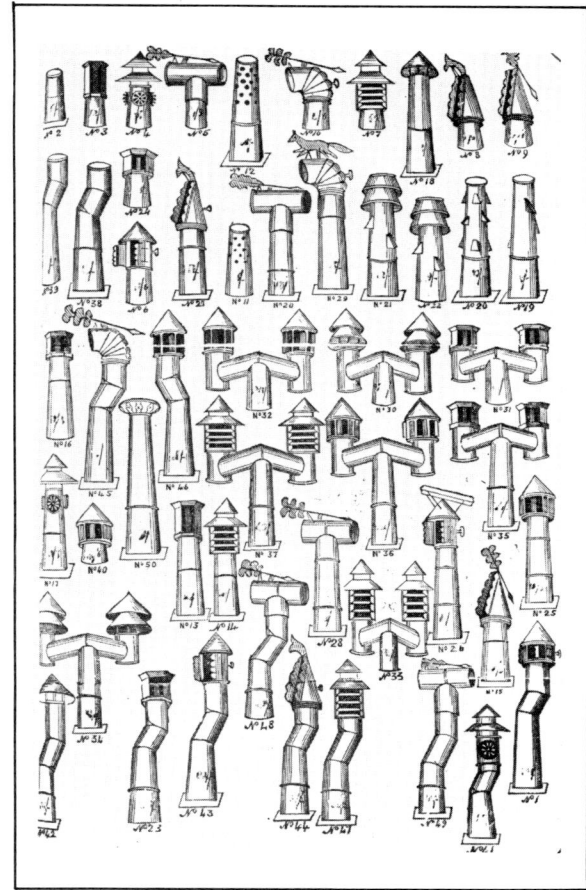

Chimney cowls from the 1860s, made by Mark Berry of Sydney and advertised in Sands' Sydney Directory *for 1861*

of the British National Clayware Federation contained nearly 500 varieties of chimney pot, the majority of which had been in production for a century or more. This great diversity was echoed, although not fully reproduced, in Australia.

The connoisseur of chimney pots, travelling through an Australian suburb developed in the nineteenth century, will observe a surprising number of different types of pots and may also find an occasional chimney cowl. Cowls are comparatively rare as they were made from metal and have largely been discarded owing to the ravages of rust. A metal fin caught the wind and blew the cowl around so that smoke and gases moving up the flue were ejected from the chimney in the direction in which the wind was travelling. The action of the wind moving past the cowl was intended to create suction and increase the updraught in the flue. Cowls were developed to overcome problems resulting from downdraughts or high pressure zones at the top of chimneys.

Chimney pots are not mere ornaments but make a significant contribution to the overall efficiency of a domestic fireplace and chimney system. Their shape tapers towards the top, and serves to increase the velocity of escaping smoke and gases, and to strengthen the updraught. The comparatively small outlet area at the top reduces to a minimum the area acted upon by the wind, lessening the effect of downdraughts and minimising the entry of rainwater.

Chimney pots made to patterns introduced around the turn of the twentieth century are still manufactured in Australia. Several designs are available from the Sydney firm of Fred A Mashman Pty Ltd. Fred Mashman's pots are suitable for both late Victorian and Edwardian houses. More elaborate pots made to earlier designs can be obtained at demolition sites or from dealers in secondhand building materials. Chimney pots are handmade by skilled potters and their manufacture impedes the production of more profitable clay products which occupy less space in the kilns. British potteries which were still making chimney pots until quite recently include Red Bank Products of Measlam, near Burton-on-Trent, Doulton's of Wilnecote near Tamworth, Wragg's of Swadlincote, the Kinson Pottery at Parkstone, and Cumberworth's in Yorkshire.

HARDWARE

The hardware originally fitted to Victorian and Edwardian houses is a rich and fascinating subject for study, providing in its development over the years an insight into technological change in one of industry's more creative and innovative periods. In Britain the products of Victorian manufacturers were regarded with an uneasy blend of patriotism and contempt. Many people with a well developed aesthetic sense regarded mass produced items with suspicion, distrust and dislike. There was a widespread feeling that only human hands could create objects with any claim to artistry or quality of design. Eyes used to medium-grade products of the late twentieth century can see qualities in Victorian or Edwardian hardware that were perhaps not apparent to all at the time of its manufacture.

The metals most commonly used were mild steel, cast iron, brass and copper. From these humble materials the manufacturers of architectural and builders' hardware produced a great range of items that were often both functional and decorative. As Charles Eastlake wrote in 1868: 'There is, perhaps, no branch of English trade more prolific in design than that of the furnishing ironmonger.'[21]

There were locks and keys, bolts, picture hooks, finger pulls, sash weights and fasteners, grates, gasoliers, screws, nails, hinges, shutter flaps, fanlight openers, door knobs, handles, knockers, chains and stoves, of many types and sizes. Some of these items are of such importance to the restorer that they are treated individually elsewhere in this book. The wealth of architectural hardware used in Australia between 1840 and 1910, some of it locally made but much imported from Britain, is such that only the most superficial examination is possible here. A brief inquiry into one item of hardware will serve to illustrate the complexity of this subject.

FANLIGHT OPENERS

Iron or brass fanlight openers were the subject of numerous patents during the 1880s and 1890s. Inventive minds produced many mechanical gadgets to open and close the small horizontal windows or fanlights which were a normal feature above front and many internal doors. Their name was derived from the fan-shaped windows or 'lights' which were introduced to domestic architecture prior to the Victorian period. Eventually, any window above a door became known as a fanlight. Most houses had fanlights above the front door, French doors, and the doors to the dining and drawing rooms, and major bedrooms.

Fanlights served a very useful purpose, providing fresh air in a flow which could be very carefully controlled without at the same time leaving the house open to easy access by intruders. In most unrestored houses they have been inoperative for many years, and are usually found to be stuck fast by numerous coats of paint. The mechanical contrivances used to open them, the subjects of patents by such inventors and manufacturers as Wollensak, Beanland, Adams, McPherson, Simplex, Hills and Ross, have either been painted solid or discarded. Fanlights were also sometimes operated by a cord system.

Fanlight openers were occasionally made of brass but in most cases the metal preferred was mild steel because of its greater strength. They were often finished in black but were also available in finishes described as copper bronzed or antique coppered. Replacement of missing fanlight openers is a matter which can only be treated in accordance with the individual circumstances. Clues to the original presence of a mechanical fanlight opener will usually be found in marks on the woodwork of the fanlight itself or the doorframe. The only source of supply known to the author is demolition sites.

As so many different brands were available within a comparatively short period of

time and the subject has still not been researched, it is difficult to provide clear guidelines for those people who would like to insist that an 1880s house should be refitted with fanlight openers that were available at that time. Most will be content with finding fanlight openers that will do the job while providing a feeling of reasonable authenticity.

BRASS AND IRON

As for the other items of architectural hardware which were fitted to houses of this period, it can safely be said that brass and cast iron were the metals most favoured. Both were easy to cast and produced objects that were pleasing to the eye as well as being reasonably priced. In all its varied forms the brasswork of Victorian houses provided useful employment for generations of maids. As changing economic and social conditions ended the era of domestic staff, the glory of polished brass began to fade in the inner urban areas of Australia's larger cities and towns. In time, most of the tarnished brass was painted or discarded. Rising costs and developments in manufacturing techniques ultimately resulted in the use of other metals which were used to produce cheaper and less durable hardware.

A house which has been stripped of most of its architectural hardware over the years should be carefully surveyed in order to determine what is required for this aspect of its restoration. It will often be found that enough individual items are left, perhaps scattered in rooms throughout the building, to provide a complete or nearly complete picture of its original fittings. Secondary rooms such as bedrooms may provide enough items to equip the major rooms where such details are essential to a meticulous restoration. Others can often be found at demolition sites, or occasionally, at antique or junk shops.

Contemporary houses, especially those close to the building being restored, often provide clues to the type and style of objects that are missing. In situations where only one example of a particular item can be found–such as a brass finger pull for a window—and several are required, new ones can be cast to match. Some items of hardware, including sash fasteners, are still available in old-fashioned styles from suppliers of quality architectural hardware in the major cities.

Cleaning heavily tarnished and encrusted brasswork is a task that some people enjoy and others prefer to pass on to a professional brass polisher. A higher and perhaps less-authentic polish is obtained from the professionals who also add a clear lacquer or varnish which is intended to eliminate any further need for polishing. The purists say that hand-polished brass acquires a patina that no machine can give. But whatever the process employed there is no doubt that the soft glow of polished brasswork adds great appeal to the atmosphere of a well-restored house.

LOCKS

Old locks are a neglected industrial art-form, antiques which few dealers or collectors have begun to appreciate. Disinterest appears to be very largely due to the lack of understanding of the processes by which their original function and beauty can be restored.

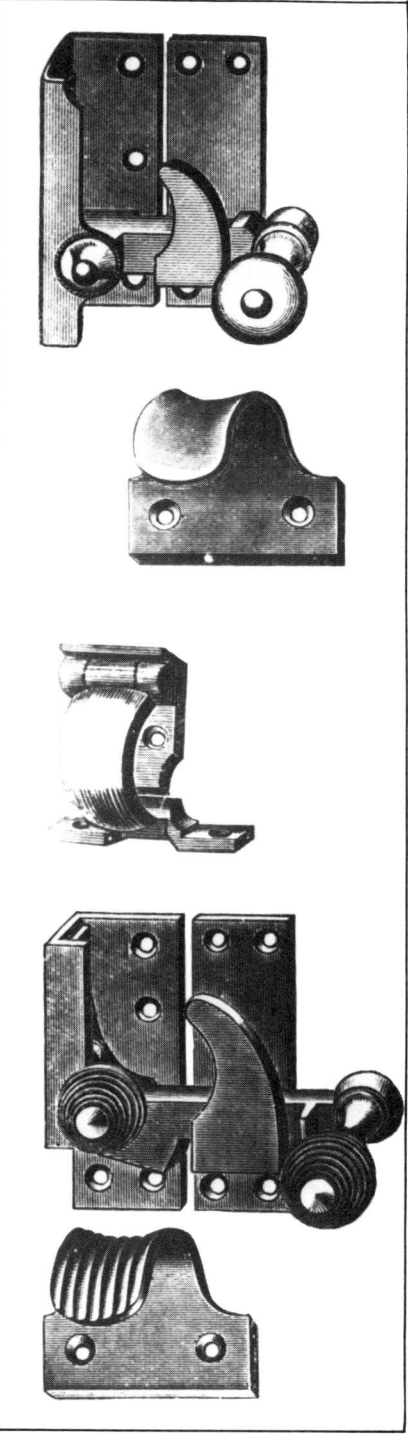

Brass and iron and window furniture, from the 1909 catalogue of F Lassetter and Company of Sydney

The escutcheon for a Vaughan drawback rimlock, often to be found on an old front door after the lock itself, right, has long been removed

DOOR FURNITURE.				149

Handles, china, amber and crystal, p. pair 4s. 6d. to 20 0
Brass door hooks, per inch 0 4½

CARPENTERS' PATENT RIM LOCKS.

5 in.	6 in.	7 in.	8 in.	9 in.	10 in.
3s. 2d.	3s. 6d.	4s. 3d.	5s. 9s.	10s.	15s.

Improved furniture for ditto 15d. to 20d. per set

IMITATION DITTO.

5 in.	6 in.	7 in.	8 in.	9 in.	10 in.
2s.	2s. 3d.	2s. 9d.	4s.	6s.	7s. 6d.

FINE WARD DRAW-BACK LOCKS.

	7 in.	8 in.	9 in.	10 in.	12 in.
Common ..	.. 4s.	5s.	6s.	8s.	11s.
Better.. ..	.. 5s.	6s. 6d.	8s.	9s. 6d.	15s.

MORTICE SASH LOCKS, *with brass furniture, each.*

	s. d.		s. d.
4 inch ..	.. 4 0	6 inch ..	.. 6 0
5 inch ..	.. 5 0	7 inch ..	.. 7 0

If rebated, add 25 per cent.

MORTICE IRON LOCKS, *with crank furniture, each.*

1¼ in.	1½ in.	1¾ in.	2 in.
4s.	4s. 6d.	5s.	6s.

If rebated one-half more.

	s. d.
MORTICE SASH LATCHES, with furniture complete from	3s. to 4 0
CABIN BRASS LOCKS each	7s. 6d. to 8 6

SASH FURNITURE.

	s. d.
Sash fastenings, burglar proof, each ..	10d. to 1 3
Sash fastening and screws, ditto, ..	6d. to 4 6
Spring roller ditto, ditto	1s. to 2 0
Cranked ditto, for casements, ditto ..	1s. 6d. to 3 0
Sash centres or pivots, per pair ..	6d. to 1 0
Best or patent sash line, per yard ..	0 1½
Copper sash line, per lin. foot ..	3d. to 1 0
Sash weights, iron, per lb.	0 1½

From the Australian Builders' and Contractors' Price Book, *1886*

Where old locks are available in antique shops they are seen either unrestored and hence very shabby, or else their surface has been ground back to bare, shining metal and coated with clear lacquer. In neither case are they very appealing. It is seldom that they are offered complete with their keyhole escutcheon or the all-important staple which fits on the door-jamb and makes their function as locks possible. Original keys are also rare.

It is hardly surprising that this bad presentation has failed to create public interest or demand. Properly treated and well restored old locks add interest and appeal to a Victorian or Edwardian house. Certainly, no restoration project can be regarded as complete until period locks, in good working-order and appearance, have been fitted to the building. They should of course be accompanied by the appropriate door furniture.

The vast majority of the locks made in the Victorian era were rimlocks; they sat on the surface of the door at its edge or rim. Mortice locks began to appear at a later date and became increasingly popular in the Edwardian period, especially in houses of superior quality.

The English manufacturers, Carpenter and Vaughan, produced most of the locks fitted to Australian houses in the eighty years prior to World War I. Their products were shipped to Australia in great numbers and, in the absence of any significant local competition, met with an eager response. Of the two firms, that of James Carpenter is the older and better known. Carpenter's first lock patent was taken out in association with John Young on January 18, 1830, when the lockmaking industry was still in its infancy.

Like Henry Ford's first cars, James Carpenter's rimlocks were available in any colour you liked provided that was black. The standard finish was black japan. Josiah Parkes' *Encyclopaedia of Locks and Builders' Hardware* describes it:

> … black bright japan, which is sometimes called varnish, is used extensively for finishing the iron and steel cases of rim and other locks. This provides an attractive finish and valuable protection against corrosion. Dipping and spraying are the usual ways of applying it, after which the articles are dried in a stove.[22]

This finish is occasionally seen in a wrinkled form. The series of Vaughan locks which were manufactured with ornate cast-iron cases were sometimes finished with brown varnish, an alternative to japan which imparted a faint coppery glow to the metal.

Restoration of old locks can be time-consuming but is a very rewarding process. As few of them come complete with original keys, it is often necessary to seek out one of the small number of locksmiths who still have stocks of the old-fashioned blanks which are required to cut new keys. Replacing missing or broken springs is a comparatively simple matter but where other parts are absent or broken the services of a lockmaker may be needed to replace them. Large manufacturing companies are not likely to be of assistance. Help should be sought from one of the few lone exponents of the lockmaking trade

A Vaughan rimlock of the type used on internal doors in Victorian and Edwardian houses. A very similar lock was made by the rival firm of James Carpenter

or the smaller firms which are prepared to take an interest in such unusual projects. It is advisable to obtain an estimate of the cost as such specialised skills are often expensive.

As most old locks are covered with a thick coating of paint, the first step in restoring them is to remove all surface coatings and reveal the surface of the metal. They should be carefully taken apart and the cases and staple cleaned with paint-stripper or caustic. Screwdrivers, a wire brush, emery paper, fine file and rag are the major tools and materials required. Small screwdrivers or sharp, pointed knives may be used for cleaning dirt and paint fragments from corners and crevices. The dust and dirt of generations should be removed from inside the case and all component parts removed and cleaned. All rust should be cleaned from moving parts and springs which can then be lightly smeared with fine oil.

The original finish to the lock's case is likely to be removed during cleaning but is easily replaced. When the case has been cleaned back to bare metal it should be treated with a rust inhibitor or metal primer and finished with black japan. Several coats of Blac-It, another traditional finish of the Victorian era, provide a suitable alternative to japan. Both Blac-It and black japan are available from the suppliers listed in the 'Directory', page 130.

The cast-iron range of Vaughan locks may be coated with either brown or clear varnish to provide a finish which is very close to the original. Brass components should be polished and may be lacquered to prevent future tarnishing.

Front door locks are larger than locks fitted to internal doors and, because of the sliding action of the bolt, are known as drawback rimlocks. Locks of this type manufactured by Carpenter are usually large and substantial, with heavy brass knob and fittings, and a weighty bridge-ward key. They were available in standard sizes of eight inch, ten inch and twelve inches in length (200, 250 and 300 mm). Vaughan drawback rimlocks are often smaller and more delicate, and feature intricate patterns on the cast-iron case and staple. They were available as double-throw locks, a type which Josiah Parkes describes as having '. . . a dead bolt which, after the first throw, can be shot out further by an extra turn of the key'.[22]

The front door will usually present several clues to the style, size and even the brand of lock that was first fitted to a house. In some cases the original lock will still be mounted on the door, but rendered inoperative and with its function taken over by a more modern lock. In most cases a locksmith will be able to repair it although replacement of missing or broken components may involve a search through demolition yards or at demolition sites.

Where the front door lock is missing its size and shape should be discernible in the pattern of the paint on the inside of the door. The original key escutcheon is often still in place on the outside face of the door but is usually buried beneath many layers of paint.

SAXTON & BINNS, LTD.
IRONMONGERY—Continued.

Door Knobs, Bronze, from	...	...	each	1/6 to 6/-
Door Knockers, from	...	...	,,	1/6 to 6/-
Fanlight Openers, Bronze ...	...	...	,,	2/-
,, ,, ,,	...	...	,,	3/-
,, ,, ,, ...	...	...	,,	4/-
,, ,, Nickel plated	...	...	,,	6/-
,, ,, ,,	...	...	,,	8/-
Sash Fasteners, Bronze ...	...	...	,,	5d
,, ,, Brass and China	...	...	,,	10d
,, ,, ,,	...	...	,,	1/3
Sash Lifts, Brass ...	...	...	,,	1/6
,, ,, ,,	...	...	per doz.	3/6
Sash Line, No. 3 (Anchor)	...	...	,,	5/-
,, ,, 4 ,,	...	...	per gross	6/6
,, ,, 5 ,,	...	...	,,	7/6
,, ,, 6 ,,	...	...	,,	10/6
				12/6
(Special Make and Quality Lines quoted on application.)				
Sash Weights, Best Scotch	...	...	per cwt.	8/6
,, ,, ,,	...	...	per lb.	1d
Sash Pivots for Fanlights...	...	...	per doz.	3/-
Screws, 1in. ..	...	...	per gross	10d
,, 1¼in. ...	...	..	,,	1/2
,, 1½in. ...	...	...	,,	1/5
,, 2in. ...	...	...	,,	1/9
,, 2½in. ...	...	...	,,	2/3
,, 3in. ...	...	...	,,	3/6
Register Grates, 36in., from	...	...	,,	15/-
Colonial Ovens, from	...	...	each	12/6
Centre Flowers, Cast Zinc, 18in.	..	...	,,	4/6
,, ,, ,, 24in.	...	...	,,	8/6
Verandah Frieze (Cast Iron), from	..	...	per foot	9d
Do. Brackets, from ...	...	...	each	3/-
Designs and Prices for Cast Iron Verandah Finishings on application.				

27

SAXTON & BINNS, LTD.
IRONMONGERY.

Butt Hinges, Cast Iron, including Screws, 2½in., per doz. pairs							4/-
,, ,, ,, ,, 3in.	,,	,,					4/6
,, ,, ,, ,, 3½in.	,,	,,					5/-
,, ,, ,, ,, 4in.	,,	,,					6/-
Tee Hinges, strong, including Screws, 10in.	,,	,,					6/-
,, ,, ,, ,, 12in.	,,	,,					7/-
,, ,, ,, ,, 14in.	,,	,,					8/-
,, ,, ,, ,, 16in.	,,	,,					10/-
,, ,, ,, ,, 18in.	,,	,,					11/-
Hook and Eye Hinges, strong, 18in.	...		per pair				4/-
,, ,, ,, ,, 24in.	...						5/3
Parliament Shutter Hinges and Screws			per pair, from				1/3
Brass and other Hinges quoted for on application.							
Locks, 4in. American Rim, Mineral, Furniture		..	each				1/3
,, 6in. Rim, Brass Furniture	...					,,	2/-
,, 7in. ,, ,, ,,	...					,,	2/9
,, 7in. Drawback ,, ,,	...					,,	4/6
,, 8in. ,, ,, ,,	...					,,	5/-
,, 6in. Carpenter's Rim, Brass Furniture	...					,,	4/-
,, 7in. ,, ,, ,, ,,	...					,,	5/-
,, 8in. ,, ,, ,, ,,	...					,,	7/-
,, 7in. ,, Drawback ,,	...					,,	5/6
,, 8in. ,, ,, ,,	...					,,	6/6
,, Mortice, English make	...					from	3/-
Mortice Lock, Furniture, quoted on application.							
Barrel Bolts, 6 in. Iron,	...	...				each	7d
,, ,, 8 in. ,,	...	...				,,	9d
,, ,, 5 in. Brass	...	...				,,	1/4
,, ,, 6in. ,,	...	...				,,	2/3
Bolts and Nuts, Cup-headed, 4in. long and upwards			per lb.				4d
Axle Pulleys	...	...			from per doz.		2/6
Axle Pulleys, Brassfaced and Kenricks, quoted on application.							
Shutter Flaps	...	...				each	7d

26

From the catalogue of Saxton and Binns Ltd, Sydney, 1905

Drawback rimlocks by Carpenter used oval escutcheons cut from thin sheets of brass. The use of a Vaughan cast-iron lock on a front door will be indicated by the highly individualistic escutcheons of cast iron, decorated with a raised pattern set against a ribbed background. The period of manufacture of many of the Vaughan cast-iron locks can often be determined by means of the diamond and circle pattern on the back of the case—see details of design registration on page 30.

Knobs fitted to internal doors furnished with rimlocks in the style patented and popularised by Carpenter and later adopted by Vaughan were invariably of brass. These are usually badly battered and can be replaced by new brass knobs and escutcheons which are still available in the same style today.

Demolition sites and contractors are the best source of supply for old locks. The purchaser should try to obtain the lock, staple and keyhole escutcheon. In some cases it may be necessary to buy a door in order to obtain the desired lock and its fittings. The use of these fascinating examples of the skill of early locksmiths and manufacturers is likely to increase in the future as more people become aware of their unique appeal.

FINGER PLATES

Fingerplates of porcelain, and later of brass, bronze or wood, were used to decorate the internal doors of Victorian and Edwardian houses, and to protect the paint or varnish from discolouration and dirt. Their survival rate has not been high as porcelain was easily fractured and they were unfashionable for many years. Applied design was minimal in most cases except towards the end of the Edwardian period when raised or indented patterns were the rule for the metal fingerplates then in vogue.

Victorian fingerplates were of black or white porcelain, usually adorned with simple patterns in gold. In most cases the decoration consisted of a gold line or band around the perimeter of the plate but examples of fingerplates decorated with ferns or other motifs have been found. In 1892, the Sydney hardware merchants, W C Fallick and Sons, carried a range of finger plates which included 'a series on which are painted specimens of Australian flora, such as the waratah, the flannel-flower etc. beautifully executed for the firm by Messrs Lyon, Wells and Cottier',[23] a Sydney firm described as 'art decorators and glass-stainers'.[24]

Fingerplates should be positioned in the rooms which are being restored in accordance with the original character and decoration of the rooms. Doors leading to other rooms from the traditionally dignified and sombre entrance hall should be furnished with black fingerplates. The door to the drawing room may have a black fingerplate facing the hall and a white plate in the drawing room. Where folding doors divide the drawing room from the dining room, white fingerplates should face into the drawing room when the doors are closed while the other side of the doors will be furnished with black plates. The masculinity of the dining room was emphasised by its dark marble fireplace and black fingerplates. The rule is by no means universal and appears to have been interpreted with some flexibility, perhaps as a result of uncertain supplies. Antique black fingerplates are rare and even white plates in the correct shape are difficult to obtain.

Where gold decoration has faded or been worn away it may be replaced, if desired, by a careful hand using a fine brush and gold paint. The use of adhesive tape will greatly assist in painting the straight lines of the decoration. A clear lacquer may be used to protect the paint from fading and wear. Retouching fingerplates should be avoided as it is desirable to retain the patina of age.

Where fingerplates were originally fitted to an old house but have since been removed their shape and position may still be located on the doors. An oblique light will often indicate patterns on the paint, beneath which will be found the putty-filled holes for the

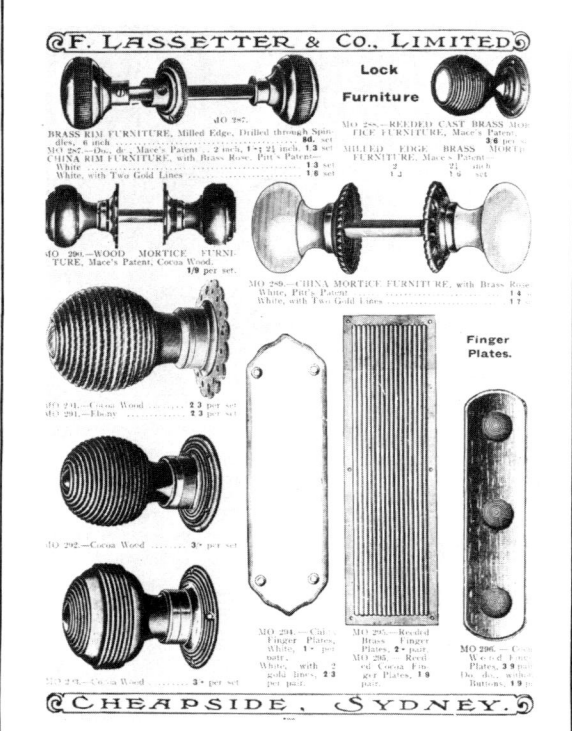

Finger plates and door knobs, from the catalogue of F Lassetter and Company, Sydney, 1909

screws which held the original plates. Miniature fingerplates were occasionally fitted to doors in houses occupied by families with young children. These were positioned beneath the lock on both sides of the doors.

Replacement fingerplates may be obtained from demolition sites, antique dealers or from the Melbourne hardware store of N J Reid, whose address is listed in the 'Directory', on page 126. This firm imports new fingerplates made to authentic nineteenth-century patterns. The fingerplates which are at present available from many hardware stores are not suitable for restoration purposes.

When buying fingerplates it is generally advisable to obtain one or more spares. Care should be taken when fitting fingerplates as the last turn of the screw is often the one that cracks the porcelain.

BELLS

Middle- and upper-class Australian households in the period covered in this book were staffed by servants as a matter of course. Their role is often forgotten and their previous presence in homes which are today neglected and dilapidated, in areas which are perhaps now low on the social scale, may be difficult to imagine. 'The servant problem' was a conversational topic of which employers never tired, but only when the cook or house-maid was safely out of earshot. The problems faced by the well-to-do in New South Wales in the mid-1840s, a few years after the cessation of convict transportation, are described by Colonel Godfrey Mundy in *Our Antipodes*:

> . . . a cook,—in the solemn signification of the word—is in New South Wales a fabulous animal—fabulous as the Bunyip of the blacks. The mencooks are mostly ship-cooks, or stewards, dealers in cocky-leaky, seapie, plumdough, and other bluewater barbarisms. The shecooks are kitchenmaids at best.[25]

The great majority of suburban houses in Australia, including medium to large terraces and cottages, would have been staffed by a cook/housekeeper with perhaps a housemaid who was often a young girl. By 1917 it was being said that 'the services of one maid is the most that the wife of the ordinary man can have, and often enough even this help cannot be afforded'.[26] Evidence of the presence of servants can be clearly seen today in most of the comfortable larger terraces built in inner urban areas of our cities and towns.

The most positive indication that a house was built to be run by servants is the system of bells with which they were summoned to the various rooms or to the front door. All but the humble cottages of working men were fitted with a bell system, the installation of which was carried out by specialist tradesmen. With the passing of the era of domestic servants the bells fell into disuse and today very few buildings retain a complete system. It was seldom, however, that property owners took the trouble to strip the buttons, wires and bells from throughout the house. Over the years pieces of the system were removed when they were damaged, or during alterations, repairs or re-decoration.

Both mechanical and electrical bell systems are to be found. The mechanical system is earlier and consisted of copper wires sliding through zinc tubes. When the fitting at the point of origin was pulled a small bell tinkled in or near the kitchen. Bells were of brass or an alloy of four parts copper to one part tin. As each bell had a different note, servants immediately knew to which part of the house they had been summoned. The architect George Robson provided a neat description of the bells in *Modern Domestic Building Construction*, published in 1876: 'Each bell is to be of the best bell-metal, of good and distinctly different tone, the one from the other, mounted on best plate carriages,

Bells in the servants' hall at Retford Park, Bowral, N S W, built in 1887

SERVANTS WANTED

NEEDLEWOMAN wanted, to assist in house; knowledge Willcox & Gibbs' m. Miss Thynne, 100, King-st.

WANTED, a middle-aged WOMAN, to assist in housework; a comfortable home. 128, Prince-street.

WANTED, Cooks and Laundresses (Protestants), and General Servants. Mrs. Bradford, 126, Castlereagh-st.

WANTED, a single Man, as COOK. P. M'Carroll, Redfern.

WANTED, a MAN, to drive a horse. Apply New Market Hotel, Campbell-street.

WANTED, a General SERVANT. Two doors from Bishopthorpe-terrace, Glebe Road.

WANTED, a useful GIRL. Apply after 9 a.m. at 334, Liverpool-street, Darlinghurst.

WANTED, an active BOY, to be generally useful Poppenhagen's Hotel, Clarence and Barrack sts.

WANTED, a strong active Girl, as General SERVANT. 25, Bank-street, Chippendale.

WANTED, a Nurse-Girl, handy with needle. Apply between 2 and 4, at Mr. Callaghan's, 306, George-st

WANTED, a GIRL, to nurse and be useful. Kent House, Kent and Bathurst streets.

WANTED, a young Man as PORTER. None need apply without reference. A. Conway, jeweller, Geo -st.

WANTED, a good General SERVANT. 235, Kent and Margaret streets.

WANTED, a young Man, as BOOTS; reference required. Apply Post Office Hotel, York-street.

WANTED, a thorough General SERVANT. Apply at the Clarendon Hotel, George-street.

WANTED, a COACHMAN. Apply at 190, Macquarie-street.

WANTED, a MAN, to break up bush land. Apply 178, Sussex-street, before 9.

WANTED, a LAD, used to a butcher's shop. F. Allen, Pitt-street, Redfern.

WANTED, a General SERVANT. Apply at Mr. Cooper's, Brown-st., Newtown, off Missenden Road.

WANTED, General SERVANT, for small family. Apply at 62, Yurong-street, Woolloomooloo.

WANTED, for Goulburn, a young Woman as NURSE. Apply 156, Alberto-terrace, Darlinghurst Road.

WANTED, a MAN and strong BOY to make themselves generally useful. Smith's coal yard, Crown-st

WANTED, a General SERVANT, must be a good Laundress. 115, Lankelly-terrace, Macleay-street.

WANTED, a GIRL—housework. Sleep at home if preferred. 193, Bourke-street, near William-street.

WANTED, a HOUSEMAID. Apply Mrs. Macintosh, Lindsay. Darlinghurst.

WANTED, to accompany a lady to Morpeth, competent House and Parlour MAID. 309, Castlereagh-st.

WANTED, a steady, sober young MAN, used to the butchering. H. Quinlan, Market-street.

WANTED, a middle-aged WOMAN. Henry Rice, butcher, Elizabeth-street, Haymarket.

WANTED, a General SERVANT. Plough Inn, George and Liverpool streets.

From the Sydney Morning Herald, *12 May 1870*

with scrolls, spring-pendulums, and labels, with the names of the various rooms, &c, inscribed thereon . . . .'[27]

The work of the bellhanger is described in Colonel H C Seddon's *Builder's Work and the Building Trades* in 1889:

The bell-hanger provides and hangs the bells required for communicating between the different parts of a building, and connects them with their pulls, or handles, by means of cranks and wires.

The action of the pull upon the bell should be as direct, and effected with as few cranks as possible; and the cranks and wires should be concealed from view, both to protect them from injury, and on account of their unsightly appearance. In all superior work the wires are conducted along concealed tubes, fixed to the walls before the plasterer's work is commenced. The simplest way of arranging the wires is to carry them up in separate tubes to the roof, where they may all be conducted to one point, and brought down a chase in the walls to the part of the basement where the bells are hung. By this means very few cranks are required, and a broken wire can be replaced at any time without trouble.

Bell-hanger's work is paid for by the number of bells hung; the price being determined by the manner in which the work is executed. The furniture to the pulls is charged in addition, at per piece.[28]

In earlier times the great houses of the colonial gentry were fitted with elaborate systems, operated by the manipulation of richly decorated bell-pulls. James Bowman, Inspector

of Colonial Hospitals in New South Wales, imported bell-pulls from England for his mansion, Lyndhurst, at Glebe. Bowman's dining-room was fitted with 'rich crimson silk and worsted bell ropes with tassels and rosettes'. These were sent from London in 1835.

Electric bells became popular in the latter part of the nineteenth century. They were normally battery powered and were actuated by buttons at the front door, in the dining and drawing rooms, and in the main bedrooms. The front-door button was set in a rosette, usually of brass or porcelain, fixed to the wall adjacent to the door. Inside, the buttons were set in small domes which were usually fixed to the edge of the chimney breast near the top of the mantelpiece. When the button was pressed the circuit was closed and a bell rang in the servants' quarters. This type of system incorporated a board which indicated the room where service was required.

Where a house has been fitted with bells, restoration of the system is desirable, at least in part. As the bellhanger has long since vanished from the ranks of Australian tradesmen the repair of a mechanical system can be undertaken by a home handyman. Missing fittings may be obtained from antique shops or demolition sites. Repairs to an electrical system may be easier and will generally involve cleaning tarnished contact points in the buttons, replacing wires and cleaning and overhauling the bell-case. Where the case is missing the task becomes more difficult and may involve a long search in antique shops and at demolition sites. Some owners may decide to restore the system in appearance only as a fully operational network of bells will never again summon anyone from the long-vanished army of domestic servants.

Decoration

Victorian cast-iron decoration was frequently painted in dark colours to contrast with the lighter shades used on the walls of the house. Deep bronze green, deep Brunswick green or deep Indian red are suitable

The restoration of old houses should be carried out in much the same way as the restoration of antiques. What is missing should be replaced, exactly as it was originally but without losing the feeling of age. Few people would be foolish enough to try to 'improve' the work of a nineteenth-century cabinetmaker or artist, or to add to the pattern of an old sampler or other piece of craftwork.

This chapter covers painting, wallpaper, lighting, decorative tiles, cast iron and glass.

PAINTING

A house should be re-painted in its original colours or in traditional colours of the period. Original colours can be determined by careful research on the building which involves the stripping or peeling away of later layers to reveal the original finish. The use of authentic colours will re-inforce the original character of the house and increase its value and significance as part of Australia's architectural heritage. 'There is nothing which better displays careful study and design on the part of the architect, and skilful workmanship on the part of the builder, than the painting and decorating of a building, when carried out as it should be.'[1]

Colour research is best undertaken in areas that have been protected from the sun and rain; underneath verandahs and eaves, behind columns and posts, in the recesses of window frames and in the shelter of a porch or balcony. Later paint can be burnt away or scraped off with a razor blade or other sharp instrument. Paint stripper may also be used. Care should be taken to ensure that the primer or undercoat is not confused with the finishing coat; red lead was a common first coat on walls as well as timber surfaces. It is worth noting that exterior painted surfaces may have been burnt off during the life of a building and that no evidence of the original colour will then be found. It should also be borne in mind that the effects of weathering over many years may have caused considerable fading and that the first finishing colours may have been one or two shades brighter.

Tastes in colours, as in so many other areas, have changed considerably over the years. Colours that were popular in Victorian and Edwardian times—Brunswick green, deep Indian red, Venetian red, Prussian blue, burnt sienna, verdigris, vermilion, umber and chrome yellow—were mixed on the job by tradesmen who were as skilled in making paints as they were in applying them. These colours are distinctively different and convey to eyes attuned to modern blends an atmosphere of a bygone age.

It is unusual to find that the standard colours on the cards issued by the major paint manufacturers will suit an old house. Efforts should therefore be made to locate a firm which is prepared to mix paint to order. Some firms will undertake to match colours from small samples supplied, or will prepare them in accordance with British Standard colour numbers. This system enables paints to be mixed from a written order with a high degree of colour accuracy.

From the subdivision plan of the Campsie Park Estate, N S W, 1885

Even today, painting is a trade of considerable complexity. Care should be taken when using commercial preparations, such as fillers, and special-purpose paints, such as sealers, galvanisers and non-ferrous primers, to ensure that they are applied in accordance with the directions on the package or can. Many painting tradesmen have their own special recipes for fillers, some of which contravene the manufacturers' recommendations. A typical formulation of this type involves the use of an interior or exterior filler, mixed with paint, to form what is known as Swedish putty which is widely used for exterior filling on rendered walls. It provides a smooth, flat surface and minimises the need for sanding back prior to painting. When doubts arise as to the proper application of any commercial product it is preferable to seek the advice of the manufacturer's technical department rather than relying on the advice of the staff at the local hardware store.

Preparation is of paramount importance in painting an old house. Time and effort spent on preparation will be repaid in terms of the quality of the new finish and the length of time for which it will last. A rushed effort on an unsatisfactory surface will soon begin to deteriorate. All loose and flaking paint should be removed and the surface thoroughly and properly prepared for the new coat. Where areas of existing paintwork are in good condition they may be left in position providing they do not obscure architectural detail. The edges should be feather sanded to ensure that new paintwork will blend smoothly over the old without leaving sharp lines to indicate the presence of the old paint. Various techniques may be used to remove large areas of old paint. These include burners, sanders, hand scrapers, or high-pressure water jets. Sandblasters and power-driven grinders may be used but can damage soft brickwork, mortar or render. Each method has its own particular application.

Authenticity in restoration requires an understanding of Victorian and Edwardian tastes in colour and in painting practices of the period

Where a considerable area of paint must be removed, as for example on the exterior walls of a large terrace or cottage, it is advisable to obtain quotations from contractors, not necessarily painters, who can provide reliable references. These should of course be confirmed. It may be better in the long run to pay a substantial sum for such work than for an owner to spend several weekends on such a boring and depressing task.

An aspect that is often neglected is to clean out the grooves in the stucco coating the exterior of Victorian houses. These lines are there to create the effect of the joints between stone blocks. They are often worn away or filled with paint to such an extent that the effect is virtually lost. Where the paint is loose and flaking the grooves can be readily cleaned out with a sharp scraper and re-formed where worn by the use of a masonry cutting disc, held in the hand and guided if necessary by a straight piece of light timber. The lines in awkward corners can be reached by using fragments from an old, worn disc which can be broken up for the purpose.

Each owner must make his or her own decision on how best to tackle the task of repainting. It can be undertaken entirely by contractors, by day labour, by the owner, or by combinations of these methods. Contractors will usually be found to be the fastest but the quality of the finish is not always high enough. An excellent overall result can often be obtained by using contractors for large wall areas or awkward and perhaps dangerous locations such as chimneys, while day-labour painters can be used on parts of the building where a high quality finish is required.

The drawing room at Collingwood, N S W. *The house was built over a long period but has been restored to its appearance in the 1870s*

Researching the original colours on the interior of an old house is greatly assisted if the owner knows what to expect in the areas in which he or she is looking. The entrance hall was invariably decorated in a dignified, formal manner. Wallpaper was frequently used here and is referred to elsewhere in this book. Watch for paint or wallpaper which simulates marble. The drawing room, usually the first room opening off the hall, had a light and airy atmosphere and was normally finished in pastel shades. This feminine room was separated by folding doors from the adjoining dining room with its strongly masculine emphasis and walls of deep rich reds or greens. The drawing room was in fact once the 'withdrawing' room to which the ladies retired after dinner, leaving the gentlemen to their port, cigars and lurid stories in the dining room.

Ceilings were commonly painted white or a pale shade of one of the lighter colours and were often decorated by the application of gilding or stencilled designs. Frequent repainting was necessary as gas lights generated heat and smoke which quickly caused discolouration. The conversion of homes to electricity eventually resulted in a general change to interior colour schemes. Colours which were fashionable in homes lit by gas or other nineteenth-century lighting sources were found wanting when electric light arrived.

An entrance hall with Edwardian overtones. From the Wunderlich Patent Ceiling and Roofing Company's Beautiful Homes, *Sydney, 1906*

. . . the proprietor of a mansion with a taste for the acquisition of improved scientific inventions may suddenly determine to take down his handsome candelabra or his imposing gasaliers, and substitute for them the electric light, with the result that the decorations of his apartments present, beneath its cold, bluish-white rays, a totally different appearance to that intended by their designer.

Where he would have placed delicate or pronounced warm tints as a counterfoil to the rays from an Edison or a Brush incandescent lamp, he finds he has retained cold tones, rendered still more sterile by its uncompromising searching brilliancy, and the pleasing satisfaction of knowing that he has put the right tint in the right place is denied him forthwith. Warmth of colour—which does not necessarily mean the employment of garish or overbright tones—is materially assisted by the yellow light afforded by oil lamps or by the use of gas.[2]

The following extracts are from a paper entitled 'Decoration' which was presented to the Sydney Architectural Association in 1892. The lecturer was Andrew Wells, formerly of Glasgow, but at the time a member of the firm of Lyon, Wells, Cottier and Company of Sydney. The full text of the lecture was published in the *Australasian Builder and Contractors' News* on May 7, 1892.

ENTRANCE HALL

The visitor obtains his first impression of the house on entering the hall . . . . The ceiling may be painted some shade, such as light vellum or fawn colour, or some shade of blue, neutral in tone, such as the shade presented in the duck-egg shell. The ceiling tint will be regulated by the colouring of the walls. This toning of the ceiling is good so far as it goes, but there is no limit to the various ways it may be decorated. Stencilled ornament is one of the less expensive modes. A stencil is a design cut in firm paper, cardboard, or tinfoil, and the color is stamped through the openings in the manner of printing. The cornice should be colored to connect the ceiling and walls, care being taken to use light shades where the mouldings and enrichments are delicate. The treatment as to the division of the walls will depend on the height of the ceiling, but generally speaking it is good to put a frieze under the cornice, and it is useful to have a dado here, and in the staircase following the rake of the handrail. The dado and wall space should be separated by a wooden moulded rail. The dado should be highly varnished, so as to allow of washing and dusting without the risk of soiling. The colour of the walls should be pleasantly warm, such as terracotta, or even Pompeian red, the dado in deeper shades of the wall color. The steps of stairs if of wood, should be stained a deep walnut color . . . . The hall and staircase walls may be papered—there are special designs made for the purpose that look very well indeed, having friezes and dadoes specially colored to match. The woodwork should be painted in one or more shades of maroon or other rich brown colors and varnished, all graining should be avoided.

Above left: *dining room*, Collingwood, N S W

Above: *entrance hall*, Collingwood, N S W. *Victorian and Edwardian floor coverings were usually carpet runners or squares. Adjacent floor surfaces were often painted with black japan*

The entrance hall of a large Edwardian house, from Wunderlich's Beautiful Homes *Sydney, 1906*

DINING ROOM

The dining-room should be sombre in tone, the ceiling a vellum color in depth to suit the walls. The coloring of the walls should have reference to the pictures, and should not be too light in tone; experience has discovered that dark reds or old gold color, not unlike rich brown paper or dull tones of green, either cool and grey, or warm and brown, are the best for showing pictures to advantage. As chairs are placed round the walls of the dining room, it is good to put a chair-rail at the height of the chair-backs; this prevents the chairs from breaking the plaster.

The woodwork should be painted good solid colors of Indian red or walnut shades, or black and resembling ebony. I do not recommend decorating the [door] panels with any kind of natural flower designs; thin flat hand-painted ornament in ivory color, resembling, but not imitating, inlaid work, is chaste and beautiful. If the wood is of good quality the panels may be decorated with various stains in full and rich designs. It is best to French polish surfaces decorated in this way. Both ceilings and walls may again be oil-painted and decorated in a hundred ways; I have painted many of the finest houses in Scotland in this way, the ceilings being entirely decorated by hand with figures, wreaths and ornamental compositions, the walls also being decorated with the like specially designed and hand-painted ornament. Of course, ordinary wall papers may be applied here, as everywhere else in the house, and if chosen by an expert, very fine effects may be obtained in this manner.

DRAWING ROOM

The drawing-room is the ladies' special room, and should be bright and cheerful. The dado is not so necessary here, as the chairs are not usually placed against the walls, and instead of the sombre hues suited to the dining-room, soft, quiet and light effects are best—say cream or soft duck-egg shell blue or French grey for ceilings, the wall fawn color or a richer French grey or a deeper grey blue, approaching peacock shade. All these are good for showing ladies' complexions and dress to the best advantage . . . .

The woodwork may be cream white finished with enamel varnish; this gives a beautiful smooth and fresh effect. I think the judicious application of gilding in this room very advantageous, but the same remark applies to all the public rooms and hall. I think it is better to gild the small enrichment of cornices solid than to break up the ornament of the large enrichments with points of gold—what is technically called 'hatching' or 'picking out.' The round, the concave, and small ogee mouldings always look well gilded, as their rounded surfaces catch the light from all points.

The homes of the working class or the lower-middle class in Australia were of course not decorated in the same fashion as the grand houses of Scotland, on which Mr Wells had lavished so much attention. However, his remarks were generally applicable to Australian houses although the practice of graining joinery, which he clearly did not favour, retained a strong hold in this country until well after the turn of the century.

COLOURS
This colour scheme was prepared by the Sydney restoration architects Fisher Lucas for the exterior of a house which was built in 1884. The same colour scheme would be suitable for other houses constructed in the period between approximately 1870 and 1890.

Colours have been taken from British Standard 381C. The numbers after the name of each colour provide the identification which would enable any paint manufacturer to duplicate the colours to within a very small margin of error.

WALLS	Biscuit (369), flat acrylic based.
BASE COURSE	Deep Indian Red (448), gloss.
DOOR & WINDOW FRAMES	Light Buff (358), gloss.
SASHES	Deep Indian Red (448), gloss.
LABEL MOULD TO PORCH	Deep Indian Red (448), gloss.
SIDELIGHTS FANLIGHTS DOORS	Deep Indian Red (448), gloss.
SHUTTERS	Deep Brunswick Green (227), gloss.
EAVES	Light Buff (358), gloss.
GUTTERS	Deep Brunswick Green (227), gloss.
VERANDAH WOODWORK	Light Buff (358), gloss.
VERANDAH CEILINGS	Eau de nil (216), gloss.
PORCH CEILING	White, flat.
VERANDAH ROOFS, STRIPED	Deep Indian Red (448), gloss, and Biscuit (369), gloss.
CAST IRON VALANCE, COLUMNS, BALUSTRADE ETC.	Deep Brunswick Green (227), gloss.
RAISED DETAILS ON CAST IRON	Light buff (358), gloss.
FENCE METALWORK	Deep Bronze Green (224), gloss.

A marbled architrave and doorframe. The effect was created by the careful application of layers of paint on a timber surface

GRAINING AND MARBLING

Restoration of old houses in Australia is made more difficult as a result of the disappearance or transformation of a small number of important trades. The bellhanger, for example, has gone the way of such other nineteenth-century usefuls as the coachtrimmer, waterman, cloth-cap maker, cooper, ropemaker and nailer. Painting is an example of a building trade which has greatly changed since the turn of the century. The ability to mix and prepare paint and the techniques involved in the deceptive arts of graining and marbling have been lost in a process of simplification which has rendered this trade less capable of providing the expertise which is required in restoration work. There are today very few painters with the ability to grain or marble to the standards which were common in the nineteenth century: '. . . the modern house painter can with success imitate the most varied, rare, antique, and beautiful specimens of expensive and coveted woods and marbles.'[3]

It is clear that the art of graining and marbling, both of which are important in the authentic restoration of many old houses, will quite soon be lost in this country unless a few interested tradesmen can be encouraged to acquire the necessary skills and be provided with the opportunity and incentive to practise them.

Joinery was frequently grained or marbled in Australian houses of the nineteenth century and may be seen in houses built as late as the 1920s. Graining was widely used on doors, architraves, skirting boards and staircases from the 1830s onwards. Timber mantelpieces were painted in imitation of marble as part of the overall process by means of which middle-class aspirations for the effect of affluence could be satisfied at a minimum of expense.

GRAINING   Graining has been used as an aid to decoration in Britain for about 250 years. During the nineteenth century its use became far more widespread and it was practised in the United States, Europe and the British Colonies. It is a three-part process, requiring first of all a 'ground' or basic colour which usually consists of a coat of oil paint, one or more graining coats, and a finishing coat of clear varnish. The resemblance to the recent vogue for paints that provide an 'antique' finish is no accident, although the colours and effects created by most users of this process would startle nineteenth-century painting tradesmen.

Highly skilled Victorian and Edwardian craftsmen could simulate almost any species of timber by means of careful selection of colours and the patterns created with the various brushes used by grainers; scumblers, floggers, softeners made with badger or hog's hair bristles, overgrainers, combs and combing rollers. Graining was an aspect of a trade which in the nineteenth century offered a high degree of scope for artistic expression. A good deal of practical experience was necessary in order to achieve expertise in turning pine and even cedar into such exotic timbers as mahogany, walnut, oak or bird's-eye maple.

The modern, simplified form of graining approximates to the traditional form known as brush graining and is suitable for novices as a step towards the eventual acquisition of greater skill in this deceptive art. Brush graining does not aim to simulate any particular type of wood; it merely creates an effect which enriches skirtings and architraves without a great deal of trouble or expense. In brush graining an initial coat of stain is followed by a darker coat which is patterned with the brush to create the impression of wood grain. The traditional method of graining used a new or existing coat of oil-based paint as the ground. The graining coat was applied smoothly and evenly over this and portions of it were then removed while still wet with the aid of dry brushes of various shapes and sizes, combs, rags wrapped around the finger or thumb, and even the fingertips.

Graining is only recommended for use in a house which is being restored when it is known that the original finish to the joinery was created by this process. The use of a razor blade, sharp knife or scraper will usually reveal the original finish. Graining is a technique which can only be acquired by practice. However, the following brief extract from *Graining and Marbling: A Complete and Practical Guide*, provides an indication of the processes by which Victorian and Edwardian painting tradesmen achieved their effects.[4] The extract selected is on graining in imitation of bird's-eye maple.

The ground for maple graining of all varieties is white with a creamy or yellowish cast, made up of white lead, oil, and turpentine. With a touch of lemon chrome added, and driers, this paint is applied to the door, or other woodwork to be grained in two coats. Care must be taken to ensure that one is dry and hard before the second coat is put on. Two or three days will suffice between the applications.

The graining colour is made up of two parts of raw sienna and one part of burnt umber, ground in water and made to the usual consistency with stale beer and water, or with vinegar and water. This may be applied . . . with a flat varnish brush, spreading it very sparingly in imitation of bird's-eye. When this has been done all over the panel, take a piece of thin leather, about 6 inches in length, and a couple of inches wide, hold it between your hands by both ends, and pressing it pretty hard against the work, draw it down steadily to the bottom.

By this means you produce the lights in a very natural manner. Soften it very lightly with the badger softener, and with the mottler dipped in water, draw it across between the dark spaces, and around them in some parts. Then take up your eye-dotter (a hollow-haired pencil made for the purpose), dip it in a little of the burnt sienna, and with it form clusters of very small, fine eyes, all bunched up close together and, as it were, nestling in the darker clouded places left by the leather. In this operation some grainers dispense with the use of the dotter altogether, and with the tops of their fingers dipped in the sienna colour, they dab on the eyes all over the grain. When done with speed and dexterity it looks very natural. However, the use of the eye-dotter is advisable to the beginner, until he attains more proficiency.

When dry, this class of work can be overgrained with a wash made of burnt and raw sienna in beer and water and varnished in the customary way.

MARBLING   Marbling requires a similar degree of skill to graining and the processes used are very close. In graining, a soft, textured effect is desired to simulate the pattern of timber. Marbling involves the build up of a body of solid colour with a cold, glossy surface to give the effect of the heaviness and strength of natural marble. As in graining, a close study of the material to be imitated is essential. There are many varieties of marble and as many methods of simulating it. Familiarity with the selected type is an essential first step in its creation in a few layers of paint over cheap timber. The marbler's tools include a good selection of camel-hair artist's brushes, pencils, crayons or charcoal sticks, palette, palette-knife, tubes of colour, clean rag and fine goose or turkey feathers.

Marbling was used for the walls of entrance halls and, in rare examples, on architraves. It was never seen on doors as a marble door was a practical impossibility. The aim was always to simulate reality and not to create an entirely make-believe product. A skilled marbler could, with practice, imitate almost any of the great variety of marbles that were available. The variety was more limited in Australia than in Britain but there were a few that were favourites in both countries: 'For the skirting of a staircase where marbling is introduced, Egyptian green, black and gold, or verde-antique, are the best adapted.'[5]

The colours used to create some of the better-known marbles included black, blue-black, Prussian blue, carmine, Brunswick green, yellow chrome, orange chrome, yellow

Various decorative effects and the costs of obtaining them, from the Victorian Contractors' and Builders' Price Book, *1859*

Scraping reveals the original decorative finish to the walls of a Victorian entrance hall dating from 1884. The portion of wallpaper uncovered is the frieze separating the dado from the rest of the wall.

Wallpaper from the entrance hall of Wilona, Wilona Avenue, Greenwich, N S W, c. 1900

Drawing room wallpaper of the 1840s or '50s from the Hit or Miss Hotel, Hamilton, Tasmania

The drawing room in John Brodie Spence's house, Robert Street, Glenelg, S A, photographed c. 1880. Note the wallpaper and the fan in the fireplace

ochre, Vandyke brown, ultramarine blue, Indian red, Venetian red, vermilion, scarlet lake, crimson lake, raw sienna and burnt sienna. The base colour or ground used varied according to the marble to be imitated and the preference of the individual tradesman. The ground colour was generally opaque; the effect of transparency and luminosity that is one of the characteristics of marble being created by thin coats of the colours used to imitate the marks and veins of the marble being simulated. The job was finished by the application of a fine glaze made up of the base colour thinned with mineral turpentine. This was usually applied with a feather. A coat of clear varnish was then applied.

Where marbled walls were required in the entrance hall the pattern of the 'marble' blocks was first set out and marked on the walls in crayon or pencil. Each block was then filled in with its markings and veins painted as though it were an individual piece or block of marble.

WALLPAPERS

Victorian taste in decoration can best be expressed with words such as florid, dramatic, theatrical. Taste in colour and design became increasingly extroverted in the period between 1850 and 1890. It was an outburst of decorative enthusiasm and vulgarity that perfectly suited the mood and manners of boom-time, post-goldrush Australia. Rich colours and complex patterns prevailed. Walls, ceilings and floor coverings were decorated with busy, often competing patterns. Rooms were cluttered with furniture and the furniture and mantelpieces were laden with ornaments.

Floral motifs were particularly popular for wallpapers and their cloth counterparts, the chintzes. From about 1880 onwards walls were frequently divided into three decorative zones. The lower part of the wall, from the top of the skirting board to a height of about 840 mm (33 in) was decorated with a paper of a rather bold design. A narrow frieze of paper, often printed with a classical motif approximately 125 mm (5 in) wide , separated the lower section of the wall from the main body of the wallpaper which ran to the picture rail or cornice, or to where a band of stencilled patterns flowed down from the cornice to meet it. The decorative effect continued through the cornice, the lines and patterns of which were picked out in colours or gilt, and onto the ceiling.

Ceilings in houses both grand and small were decorated with complex stencilled patterns. These were arrived at by cutting the pattern out of cardboard or similar material

A drawing room in Perth, W A. The
Edwardian wallpaper reflects the stylistic
influences of the period

Bedroom wallpaper of the 1860s or 1870s
from Morningside, Campbell Town,
Tasmania

and applying paint through the holes when the stencil was pressed flat against the surface
to be decorated. The introduction of pressed metal ceilings, patented by E H C Wunderlich of Sydney in 1888, was followed by a decrease in the use of stencilling during the
1890s.

Marble patterned wallpaper will often be found on the walls of entrance halls. It was
applied in sheets on which had been printed the patterns and 'courses' to give the appearance of marble slabs.

The Victorian style of decoration collapsed during the 1890s. The severe depression
of that decade ushered in the less exuberant Federation era with its dominant art
nouveau influences.

Careful examination of the walls of an old house may reveal some of the original wallpaper beneath later papers or several coats of paint. It is also advisable to examine the
paper at different heights in order to check for the common practice of using two or more
patterns of paper and a frieze on any given wall. An oblique light is often useful for this
purpose as it will reveal what may not otherwise be seen. Where original wallpaper is
found it should be retained, if possible, or matched as closely as possible where it has been
badly damaged, painted, or has deteriorated beyond any possibility of cleaning and
repair.

Entrance hall dado pattern from Eulbertie,
Hunter's Hill, N S W c. 1900. The paper has
a raised pattern and is known as lincrusta

Peeling paper or tears may be stuck down again with wallpaper glue. Where papers
are damaged it is worth making a thorough check for spare rolls before deciding to redec-
orate. It was common practice to place left-over rolls of wallpaper in storage somewhere
in the house. They may be found in inaccessible corners of cupboards, in the ceiling or
beneath the floor.

Stains and dirt which resist the gentle application of soap and warm water are probably best referred to an expert. A picture restorer or museum curator may be able to offer
guidance. Where it is necessary to replace old wallpaper, efforts should be made to replace
it with a new paper which is as close as possible in pattern and colour to the original.
Wallpapers made to nineteenth-century patterns are still manufactured by a small number of English firms. The names of some suppliers are listed at the rear of the book.

Where original wallpaper must be replaced a small section should be left in some
unobtrusive position to provide evidence of the house's first scheme of decoration. In
using new wallpaper the instructions of the manufacturer or supplier should be carefully
followed, particularly in regard to preparing the surface.

Handpainting tiles at the Carter Tile Company's works at Poole Dorset, c. 1900

The pottery of E Fowler and Co., Camperdown, N S W, 1864

TILES

The Victorian love of ornament is exemplified in the ceramic tiles that adorned their hearths, embellished the risers of their front steps and decorated the facades of their houses. Earthenware tiles, made by the encaustic process and known as tesselated tiles or tesserae, were used to pave their verandahs, porches, entrance halls and front paths.

The processes by which these tiles were created were perfected early in the Victorian age but it was not until the 1860s and 70s that large quantities were available for export to the Australian colonies. Ceramic tiles in particular were the result of a most effective marriage of the creative skills of British and, eventually, Australian designers, with the power and energy of Victorian manufacturers.

The encaustic process by which wax colours were painted onto earthenware tiles and fixed by means of intense heat was used by Cistercian monks in Britain and France for paving the floors of churches and castles during the twelfth century but the technique was lost during the Reformation. A version survived in the Dutch town of Delft and was taken to Britain in the seventeenth century when a few Dutch potters established themselves in Lambeth. In 1676 one Van Hamme was granted letters patent for 'makeinge tiles and porcelane and other earthenware after the way practised in Holland'. The Delftware process was quickly taken up by British tilemakers in Bristol, Liverpool and elsewhere. These delicate handpainted tiles, measuring about 122 mm (4¾ in) square by 6 or 10 mm thick (¼ or ⅜ in), continued to be produced until the nineteenth century when Samuel Wright of Shelton, Staffordshire, developed a new method based on the mediaeval manufacture of encaustic tiles. In 1830 he patented a process for the manufacture of:

> . . . ornamental tiles, bricks, and quarries for floors, pavements and other purposes. First, making these articles of fine clays, and firing them until "semi-vitrified." Second, ornamenting them in various colours and with various patterns similar to the patterns on carpets, etc, by impressing them with the patterns and filling up the impressions with clay, etc., coloured with metallic oxides. The patterns are impressed by moulding them in moulds of plaster of Paris in metal frames.

Wright's patent was sold to Herbert Minton of the firm of Minton and Boyle of Stoke-on-Trent. Minton put three men to work in a room at his earthenware works but their efforts to produce tiles met with repeated failures due to irregular contraction of the tiles, stains produced during firing, and inlaid areas that fell out at the slightest tap on the back of the tile. It was not until 1836 that Minton could be sure that all of the technical difficulties had been mastered and his first tiles offered for sale. The only colours available at first were buff, red and chocolate.

The purchase in 1840 of a half-share in a further patent, by Richard Prosser of Birmingham, was necessary to set the scene for the development of the Victorian ceramic tile industry. Prosser's idea was for the manufacture of buttons by reducing ceramic material to a dry powder and subjecting it to great pressure between steel dies. The possibilities were immediately apparent and, by late in 1840, Minton's factory was turning out white glazed ceramic tiles 150 mm (6 in) square . Other manufacturers devised processes by which tesserae, small tiles of varying shapes and sizes, were produced for laying mosaic patterns on pavements, paths and floors. Prince Albert's enthusiastic interest in ceramic tiles guaranteed success.

By 1850 tiles were being produced in great numbers for churches, mansions and public buildings. The development of transparent glazes at about this time and improved methods of production added to the appeal of ceramic tiles. They satisfied the Victorian love of ornament, providing extra patterns and visual interest in areas that had previously been bare and uninteresting. They were highly fashionable and were quickly put to use on the hearths of the houses that were springing up in the new suburbs around the cities of Britain in the 1860s and in the Australian colonies.

Prior to the development of ceramic tiles, hearths had consisted of stone slabs, approximately 150 mm (6 in) thick , scrubbed, whitened or finished with a matt-black paint. Stone continued to be used as a base for hearths until the 1890s but was eventually replaced by concrete. 'In common building the concrete is rendered on the top and trowelled off to a smooth finish, but in work of a first-class character the surface is generally formed with glazed hearth tiles, 6" by 6" [150 mm square] in size , which admit of artistic treatment, and make a sound imperishable top surface.'[6]

The first indication of the revolution in tile technology reached the Australian colonies in the 1840s and 1850s. But it was not until the 1860s and 1870s that British tiles were available in sufficient quantity for use on a large scale. Minton's lead in ceramic technology was later challenged by firms such as Maw and Co., Doulton and Co. and the Carter Tile Company which is still in operation at Poole, Dorset. There were many other British firms and a small number of Australian manufacturers. Well-known local firms included the Australian Tessellated Tile Company of Mitcham, near Melbourne; the Brunswick Brick, Tile and Pottery Company; the Sydney manufacturers, Mashman Brothers of Chatswood; Bakewell Brothers, whose factory was located at Erskineville; and the Australian Patent Tile Company of Enmore. The Fowler Potteries at Camperdown, on Sydney's western outskirts, were established in 1837 and in 1867 advertised that they could supply 'stoneware paving tiles'.[7] 'Ornamental tiles' for flooring and other purposes were produced by the Victorian Terra Cotta Lumber Company's factory at Wandong during the 1880s.[8]

The demand for fires and fireplaces in Queensland was obviously never on the same scale as in the southern states. But in 1888 Fensom's Brisbane Pottery Works on the Ipswich Road was producing large quantities of architectural pottery, including decorative tiles for the hearths of subtropical homes: 'The demand for the finer kinds of pottery produced at the works is far in excess of the supply, and this is the case with regard to fire-hobs (made in one piece) and ornamental tiles.'[9]

A tesselated tile path, c. 1880

Decorative tiles on the facade of a late Victorian house, Reserve Street, Annandale, N S W

The British manufacturers in particular vied to produce the most flamboyant and appealing patterns; birds, flowers, plants and mythological creatures. Most of the tiles seen on Australian hearths prior to 1910 were produced by a process known as biscuit printing—biscuit being the term used for tiles which had been fired once but had not been decorated or glazed. This method involved the use of a machine with engraved or etched rollers which were used to imprint a coloured pattern on fine paper known as pottery tissue. Extra colours could be added by changing the rollers and passing the paper through again, it being carefully held in register by means of fine pegs which guided it in much the same way as film is moved through a projector. The printed tissue was laid face down on the biscuit ware and pressed firmly home. Several hours later the paper was soaked off and the tiles allowed to dry before being baked. A finishing glaze could be applied by various methods including dipping, painting, fuming or vapour-glazing, or by spraying. The last stage in manufacture was to return the tiles to the kiln for the final firing which vitrified or hardened the glaze. This complex and labour-intensive operation produced an article which, although comparatively expensive, was extremely popular.

The elaborate designs which were so popular during the 1880s began to be replaced during the late 1890s by a simplified form of decoration which heralded the approach of the less opulent age which was about to begin. In Edwardian Australia there was a significant demand for tiles which expressed popular interest in native flora and fauna. This brief outburst of patriotism in the decoration of Australian homes did not survive the harsher and more practical years that were soon to arrive.

Despite nineteenth-century misgivings about the place of ceramic tiles in the world of art, there can be no doubt today of their importance and interest. They are magnificent and irreplaceable mementoes of a fascinating period and their individual value in curio and antique shops is beginning to reflect their significance. The successful restoration of a Victorian or Edwardian house may sometimes involve a long and perhaps expensive search for suitable tiles for hearths, halls, paths and verandahs.

HEARTHS

The most difficult task is likely to be that of replacing broken or missing tiles from hearths. These, because of their particular vulnerability to the impact of lumps of coal, pieces of wood or metal fenders and fire-irons, were often shattered. Where tiles are broken, but most or all of the fragments are still available, they may be pieced together and stuck down again quite successfully with a commercial tile adhesive. When a hearth is being repaired in this way all loose tiles, whether broken or not, should be firmly fixed. Tiles which can move are very likely to break. Broken tiles with fragments missing may still be utilised and the resulting gap, if filled with plastic porcelain or a similar product, is not likely to seriously detract from the overall appearance of the hearth.

Where tiles are missing or have been damaged beyond salvation the decision on how to overcome the problem is one that has to be taken in the light of the owner's dedication and available time. Seeking missing tiles of one particular colour and pattern can be a long and time-consuming task. It is, at the same time, one that can add zest to an existing interest in browsing in antique shops. Where large numbers of tiles are required, for example, in replacing an entire hearth, the task becomes more difficult but by no means impossible. The restorer has the option of simply rendering the hearth flush with the floor and painting it black in accordance with known nineteenth-century practice. This will obviate any need to seek out suitable tiles. If this is the course chosen, it is important to clean the hearth thoroughly and then gouge it with a cold chisel in order to ensure that the layer of mortar which is to replace the tiles will adhere. The addition of a suit-

able bonding agent to the mortar is advisable. This is available under various brand names from hardware stores.

Approximately twenty-six tiles are required to make up a hearth for a fireplace built around a standard 36 in (915 mm) register grate . These are laid out in a pattern of two rows, each of eight or ten tiles, with the remainder disappearing under the grate in the middle. Finding sufficient tiles, of the same pattern and, equally importantly, of the right pattern for the period of the house, is largely a matter of luck and perseverance. It is seldom that one visit to a demolition site will secure enough tiles for a hearth. In the great majority of cases tiles will be broken in removing them from the hearth in a house which is under demolition. Great care is required in removing tiles and those which are firmly secured in place will almost certainly shatter in the process of removing them. A hearth consisting of a majority of loose, unbroken tiles is a great find.

Loose tiles may best be removed with the aid of a broad, flat, scraper. The blade should be slipped beneath the edge of a tile and gently worked in until the tile comes away. Tiles which are firmly stuck to the hearth slab may sometimes be removed by using a cold chisel and hammer. Tiles which break cleanly into a small number of pieces should be kept as they can be glued together and used again. As muriatic acid will dissolve cement mortar it is possible that it may be effective in removing tiles from a mortar base.

The restorer who wishes to accumulate sufficient tiles to reconstitute a complete hearth may have to start a tile collection in order to achieve the desired goal. This method should only be undertaken if a good supply of attractive tiles is available at a reasonable price. If a demolisher can supply ten or twelve good tiles it may be worth buying them in the hope of finding enough of the same pattern to complete the hearth. Encaustic tiles for paving and ceramic tiles for hearths and decorative purposes are still available today. They can be supplied, made to order, by the firm listed in the 'Directory', page 131.

Victorian and Edwardian hearth tiles were laid close together, without the grouting which usually separates modern tiles. Hearths should be surrounded by a frame of 100 × 50 mm (4 × 2 in) pine or oregon , laid with its 50 mm edge showing, flush with the floor and mitred at the corners. This was common practice for the period and examples can be seen in most old houses. Tilers of the period worked to piece rates set by their respective associations and varied from time to time by agreement with the Master Builders' Association. In 1908, master tilers' expected 1/9d for tiling a hearth with 6 in square tiles and 2/6d for a hearth of 6 × 2 in tiles .[10] (150 × 50 mm)

'Wenger's foot-power air-compressor and vapo-aparatus for glaze-blowing'. Liquid glaze in various colours was placed in the cans marked E and compressed air released by turning the taps at C. Glazes were also applied by dipping

From the Australian Builders' and Contractors' Price Book, *1886*

Ferns in cast-iron contribute to the Australian atmosphere of this ornate Federation *terrace in Arcadia Road, Glebe, N S W*

Victorian builders and homebuyers appreciated the decorative qualities of cast-iron, despite criticism from members of the architectural elite

CAST IRON

Cast iron as a decorative material achieved its greatest popularity in Australia during the 1870s and 1880s. Its decline began in the 1890s and by 1900 its period in vogue was clearly at an end. Fashion in architecture turned then to the style that we now call Federation. With its emphasis on the use of fretted and turned wood on the facades of domestic buildings, and the adoption of Australian decorative motifs, this fashion marked the end of the Victorian era.

Attitudes towards cast iron provide a fairly accurate reflection of the changing view of architects and other middle-class groups towards Victorian housing and, by implication, towards the inner-urban areas in which such housing styles were predominant. Cast iron 'lace' was despised and scorned with an intensity which is difficult to understand today. The intellectual elite resented it, considering wrought iron to be superior because it was fashioned by hand and therefore had some claim to consideration as part of the artistic process. Criticism of the use of cast iron for ornamentation began in Australia as early as 1872, a good two decades before it began to go out of fashion: 'Cast-iron ornament is not only a sham, but the most tasteless of all shams, and the one perhaps most fatal to art.'[11]

During the 1890s architectural fashion turned to the use of timber to fulfil the role previously performed by cast iron. T A Sisley in 1890 deplored 'these birdcage frames, all frittered about with trumpery patterns, that are reared about in front of most modern villas'.[12]

The architect and lecturer, James Nangle, was among the many critics of Victorian

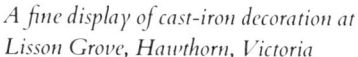

A fine display of cast-iron decoration at Lisson Grove, Hawthorn, Victoria

Cast-iron valance silhouetted between two columns, Lisson Grove, Hawthorn, Victoria

architecture whose opinions gradually filtered through the profession of architecture and into the ranks of builders, investors, and homebuyers before finally turning the tide of public opinion more than a decade after the process began. Nangle was particularly vehement about cast-iron decoration.

> . . . almost eighty per cent of recent erections in the Colonies have in some way been made to rely on this stuff for appearance, and yet . . . it would be impossible to find more than about six different designs amongst the whole. In every city and town is to be found the cast-iron shop, the keeper of which has set out on the walls the same monotonous display of specimens to be found in every other place of a like nature. He calls each design by some fanciful but totally inappropriate name. He sells it by the foot, it is put up by the foot, and the result is a never ending array of yard after yard of cast-iron, so utterly bereft of any variety or beauty, as to terribly hurt a tasteful eye, and totally stamp out even a spark of regard for cast iron.[13]

Other critics placed most of the blame on the manufacturers who were clearly responding to a vigorous market. The subject of all of this vilification would never have been sold if it had lacked appeal. By 1900, Nangle and others were urging the use of timber for decorative and practical purposes on balconies and verandahs.

> The posts may be of iron or timber. If of the former, the wretchedly over-ornamented types of cast-iron posts, or columns as they are called, which have be-

The manufacturer has cast his name into the base of the columns on this house in Goulburn, N S W

The fashion for cast-iron began to fade in the 1890s. T A Sisley, in an essay on 'The Australian Home', wrote that '. . . metal, even when skilfully wrought, is never so dignified and homelike as honest woodwork'. This house is in Goodhope Street, Paddington, N S W

come so common in Australian house-building, should be avoided, and a sensible design more in keeping with the nature of the material, adopted. Timber is, however, under ordinary circumstances the most suitable for verandah posts for even when worked so as to be ornamental this material is the cheapest.[14]

As cast iron fell from fashion, so too did the houses on which it was so profusely used. In the United Kingdom, London and other major cities were stripped of thousands of tons of cast iron which was torn from buildings in wartime to be re-cast into military hardware. In Australia, the major losses occurred when larger houses in inner suburbs were divided into small flats. Balconies which had provided a pleasant vantage point for the admiration of the urban panorama and the passing parade were enclosed and, with the installation of a sink and stove, became kitchens. They were seldom large enough to be made into bedrooms. Cracked or corroded cast iron was often discarded by uncaring homeowners or landlords who preferred the bare and incomplete effect which resulted

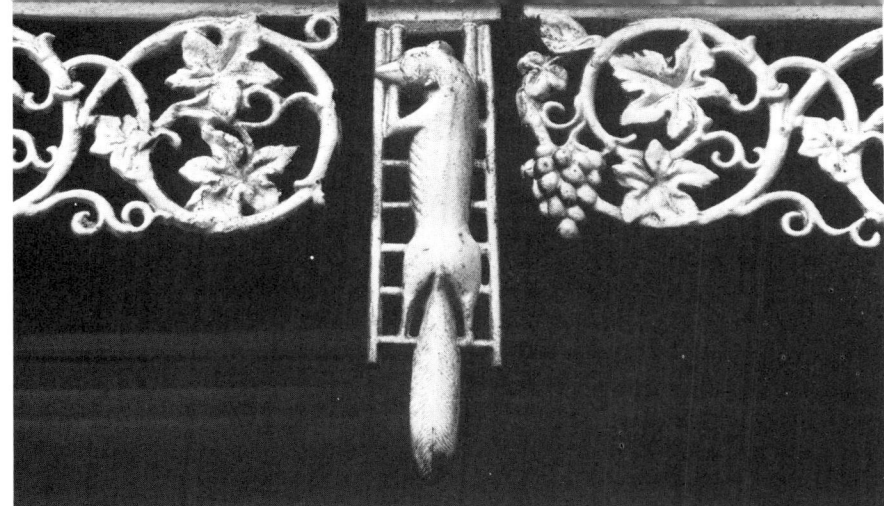

A cast-iron reproduction of an original nineteenth-century valance pattern, the fox and the grapes. The individual pieces should be butted together

to the difficulties and expense incurred in restoring their ironwork. By the 1920s no-one cared for cast iron.

H C Kent was expressing contemporary attitudes when he addressed a meeting of the Institute of Architects of New South Wales in 1924 on the subject of his experiences as a young architect and builder in Sydney in the 1870s: 'Shocking cast iron designs for balcony railings and friezes and fringes were in regular use for residential work, many examples of which still remain, at which some of you perhaps occasionally smile or shudder.'[15]

Cast iron decoration is once again in fashion. It may appear on new houses which have no other pretensions to elegance and is often incorrectly added to houses built in the Edwardian period and which have never before been adorned in this way. Although Edwardian era, or Federation style, houses are found with original cast iron combined with the predominant turned or fret-worked wood, the addition of cast iron to a house of this period is not recommended unless it is known that the house, as originally constructed, was decorated in this way.

Kyarra, *built in 1883 at the height of the fashion for cast-iron decoration, is in Madeleine Street, Hunter's Hill, N S W. A mere seven years later James Nangle wrote of '... the glaring and impudent manner in which cast-iron ornament is plastered over our buildings'.*

Paired columns contribute to the effect of the cast-iron decoration on this large house in Glenferrie Road, Kew, Victoria

Australian foundries registered many designs for cast iron between 1870 and 1900. Patterns usually differ from state to state but a few are found in several states. This cottage is in Westmoreland Street, Glebe, N S W

Iron foundries sold direct to the public or through a retailer such as the Sydney firm of F Lassetter and Company. The illustration is from their 1909 catalogue

As decorative cast iron is frequently a major feature of an old house, care and attention paid to its restoration will be fully rewarded in the overall effect created. Where all iron has been removed by a previous owner, efforts should be made to determine the pattern originally used on the building.

Fragments of a building's original cast-iron decoration may be found somewhere around the house, serving a purpose which its designers would never have contemplated. Small eaves friezes are sometimes used to retain earth in the garden while larger pieces may be located in the yard, under the house or acting as makeshift gates, fences or barricades. Cast iron found in the grounds of a house which has been stripped of its decorative iron should be closely examined in an effort to discover whether it is part of the missing iron or a stray which has been brought to the house from elsewhere.

Where no trace of the original iron can be found other houses in the area will often provide examples of suitable patterns. In the case of terraces there is usually no problem as at least one house will normally retain its iron, even in areas which have been badly run down. Houses with enclosed balconies often retain their original iron, sandwiched between layers of fibro or wood. When a decision has been made on the pattern to be used for the restoration photographs can be taken to facilitate the process of obtaining the necessary panels, friezes and pendant pieces. New reproductions in cast iron or aluminium may be available.

Antique cast iron is available from demolition contractors or dealers in antiques and building relics of the Victorian and Edwardian periods. Cast iron is also sold through the classified sections of major metropolitan newspapers. Some foundries will cast new pieces in iron or aluminium if a sample is supplied. Several are listed in the 'Directory', page 126.

In situations where the building has retained most or all of its cast iron it may be necessary to remove the iron for cleaning or repair. Sandblasting is advisable if the iron is covered with a thick coating of paint or rust but has been known to cause breakages. It is usually preferable to send the iron away for sandblasting in a workshop. It should be primed with a suitable metal primer as soon as possible after sandblasting as rusting will commence very quickly once all surface coatings have been removed. Removal of the cast iron for sandblasting or repair provides an ideal opportunity for repainting and repairs to the beams and columns to which the iron is attached.

Cracked or broken pieces of cast iron may be repaired by welding but the technique requires skill, patience and experience. A welder unfamiliar with antique cast iron can ruin a valuable piece. The casting is, generally speaking, of inferior quality and may fall apart under the stresses generated during welding unless great care is taken.

GLASS

The Victorians delighted in finding new methods of adding ornamentation to their homes. It was this zest for novelty which led them to explore the use of glass as a decorative medium. The ingenuity of the age, combined with the great demand generated by boom conditions in the building industry prior to 1890, took craftsmanship in glass to standards which have still to be surpassed in ordinary domestic glasswork. Even with the limited technology of the age, Victorian glass workers achieved effects of quite remarkable beauty. Elaborate designs were created on glass by a variety of techniques, some of which have either been forgotten or are no longer readily employed. Leadlight craftsmen and women are, with few exceptions, the only survivors of the glass decorating trade which added so much beauty to the houses of Victorian and Edwardian Australia.

Fancy glass was most commonly used at the front door of the house. It offered the owner reassurance of his place in the world and served to impress visitors and passers-by. In daylight its beauty was most apparent from inside the house. At night, the soft glow

The new sense of national identity after 1901 was reflected in the use of Australian motifs in architecture. This leadlight waratah is at 49 Boomerang Street, Haberfield, N S W

Front door panels, sidelights and fanlights in leadlight. A large house in the Italianate style, Kerribree was built in Hereford Street, Glebe, N S W, in 1889

117

Melbourne glass craftsman Keith Burley and some examples of his work

of the gasoliers or lamps provided backlighting which illuminated the porch, verandah or path.

Architects and builders were able to choose from a considerable variety of glass types, colours and methods of decoration when preparing to build a house or a row of terraces. The homes of the working classes were seldom provided with such ornamentation. Clear sheet-glass was all that could be provided for less expensive buildings. Occasionally, simple transfer patterns might be employed to add a touch of refinement to homes suitable for the more prosperous tradesmen. Middle-class housing provided the greatest opportunities for craftsmen in glass. Here, where money was freely available for ostentation, were provided the most fanciful and artful processes and designs. Leadlight, painting, transfers and embossing were utilised to provide that element of decoration which was the love of the age.

LEADLIGHT OR STAINED GLASS

The use of stained glass in windows is a craft of ancient origin. After reaching great heights of artistic expression, particularly in the windows of European cathedrals and churches, the craft faded in the fifteenth century and was not revived until early in the nineteenth century. Its possibilities for the decoration of domestic dwellings were soon recognised. The technique was brought to Australia by emigrant tradesmen and by companies which serviced the building industry.

Leadlight work involved the basically simple mechanical processes of cutting coloured glass into various shapes and holding them tightly together by means of soldered strips of lead known as cames. A degree of artistry was required where original designs were to be produced. At the peak of the industry in the last quarter of the nineteenth century, pattern books containing many designs were available. These made possible the swift production of a wide variety of standard designs which could be offered to architects or builders.

The glass used is known as antique glass. It was blown by hand and contains ripples, bubbles, veins and flecking which add character and beauty to its appearance. These apparent imperfections were no accident, as this quotation from 1888 makes clear:

> It is said, and repeated until generally believed, that glass cannot now be produced equal to the old. This . . . is not the case. All the variations and air-bubbles in the sheets, with their gradations from light to dark, which on the old windows were the result of accidents and imperfect materials, are now made intentionally; these apparent imperfections, by refracting the light, adding to the beauty and lustre of stained glass.[16]

Many different types and colours of glass were used to provide patterns, usually either geometric or representational. From 1890 onward leadlight craftsmen began to produce designs featuring Australian motifs. Art nouveau provided another very strong source of inspiration. Leadlight work is frequently seen in combination with coloured glass: ruby, blue, purple or green, not necessarily used in the same window or light but as a complementary decorative feature elsewhere in the house. Stained glass fanlights frequently featured cameo paintings. Each was a hand painted original, firmly fixed upon the surface of the glass by baking it in a kiln. Typical cameos depicted birds, fruit or flowers.

Repair or replacement of damaged leadlight is a task that should only be entrusted to craftsmen or women whose experience includes traditional patterns and who have available a good stock of suitable glass. There are many leadlight workers in the major cities.

EMBOSSED OR ETCHED GLASS

The etching or embossing of glass to form elaborate designs had its origin in the discovery of hydrofluoric acid in 1771. This unique chemical is the only acid which will corrode and dissolve the surface of glass. The decorative possibilities could not be put into effect until advances in glass making technology had resulted in the production of thicker glass in larger sheet-sizes and at a comparatively low cost.

By 1850 the inns of London and provincial cities of England featured glass worked in ornamental patterns. The process was taken up by merchants and shopkeepers and eventually flowed into domestic architecture. Some years later etched glass arrived in Australia where it quickly became established as one of the principal means of decorating the glass in and around the front doors of better quality houses. There were always critics such as the anonymous commentator who in 1888 described etching as 'that wretched travesty on stained glass'.[17] Over a period of about half-a-century an enormous range of designs was fitted to thousands of houses in cities and towns throughout Australia. Some survives today although it is clear that there has been a very heavy loss. Appropriate re-placements to damaged or broken original glass have seldom been fitted since about 1920.

Patterns in etched glass were available from stock or could be created to suit the re-quirements of the client. Popular taste in glasswork was often criticised: 'How long will our people continue to have their sense of colour . . . spoiled by miles of glaring ruby mar-gins and common blue bosses that decorate (save the mark!) our suburban residences? They are sent from England, where their use is rapidly dying out; but a large quantity is also made here.'[18]

The Victorian craftsmen who created patterns in clear glass by the use of hydrofluoric acid ran the risk of severe damage to their health. Over a long period of time it is clear that the continued use of this acid contributed to early deaths in the industry. The acid could cause very serious burns when it came into contact with the skin while the fumes given off when it was exposed to the atmosphere during etching were extremely dangerous.

Designs were created by painting the surface of the glass with a resist, often using Brunswick black, a varnish made of turpentine and asphalt, or lamp black. The glass was laid on a flat surface and a dam formed around its edge by the use of tallow or soft wax. Into this was poured the acid, diluted to one third of its full strength by adding it to two volumes of water. Those portions of the surface which had been painted with Brunswick black resisted the attack of the acid which was gingerly poured back into its container after a few minutes on the glass. Any acid left in the glass was neutralised with an alkali such as ammonia and the glass was then rinsed with cold water. The resist was removed by means of a sharp knife or scraper, and by cleansing with turps followed by soap and water.[19] (Brunswick black is a proprietary name for black japan.)

The process was generally used to eat away the surface of a design, leaving the rest of the glass sheet clear. This was the area which was initially coated with Brunswick black, with the design at that stage showing through in clear glass. Etching gave it a milky, frosted appearance and left it below the level of the surrounding glass.

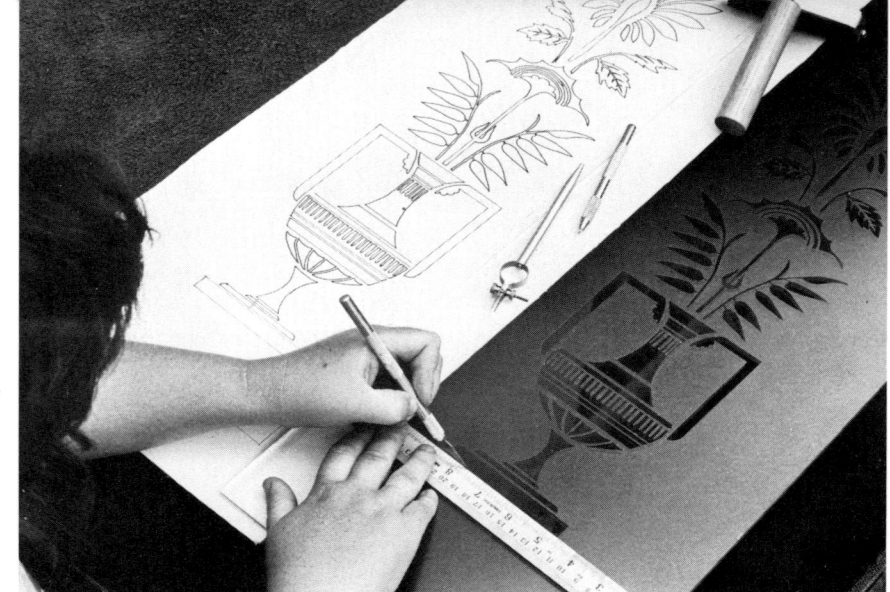

Preparing to re-create a Victorian style etched glass panel. A sheet of 6 mm clear window glass, with clear 'Con-Tact' adhesive film on its upper surface, is placed over the top of cardboard on which the design has been drawn. The design is cut out of the plastic film which is then ready to be etched. For photographic purposes the cardboard has been set to one side

After all traces of the acid and Brunswick black had been removed from the treated glass the clear area was obscured by grinding it with emery powder, moistened with water and applied by means of a flat block of copper or a slab of ground glass. The sheet of glass was bedded onto a firm, flat surface which had been protected by cloth.[19] Obscuring was hard but delicate work in which one careless stroke could ruin a design. It has been said that the real art in etching lies in the obscuring.

The replacement of etched glass will provide a challenge to the ingenuity and determination of most people who undertake the restoration of an old house. There are very few craftspeople working in this field, even in the major cities. As the complex system which supplied this type of work in Victorian times has long since disintegrated each piece of etched glass will be a special order.

The use of hydrofluoric acid in the home is not recommended and the restorer should try to locate a craftsman or woman who is willing to take on the job. As most of the labour involved in etching glass is spent on setting out the design and cutting out the resist, costs can be kept down by providing the etcher with glass which is ready to receive the acid. The best source of designs is among houses of the period of the building which is being restored, which may be located by strolling through the older suburbs of the capital cities. Where an interesting piece of etched glass is seen, it will be necessary to obtain access to the house as rubbings, after the style of English brass-rubbings, can only be taken from the interior of the building. The best results are obtained by using tracing paper and a special pencil which is composed entirely of graphite. The resulting image should be a very accurate rendition of the etching. The design can then be transferred to white cardboard in preparation for etching on a new piece of glass.

The most suitable glass for etching is clear glass, 6 mm thick. This is much thicker than ordinary window glass and provides a far more durable surface for the etching process. When used in the panels of a door it will withstand much more wear and tear than ordinary glazing. Security is also increased as six millimetre glass in small panels is difficult to break.

In one modern process, the glass is prepared for etching by placing it on top of a cardboard sheet on which the required design has been drawn. Clear adhesive plastic film (e.g. 'Con-Tact' brand) is placed on top of the glass and smoothed down firmly with a roller, removing as many air bubbles as possible. Do not prick the surface of the film to allow the air to escape because acid will enter and mark the glass. The design is now cut out of the film by means of various sharp, pointed, cutting instruments which may be obtained from specialist suppliers to artists or graphic designers. Cutting out the design is a task which requires considerable patience and skill, although the latter can be acquired as work proceeds. Depending on the complexity of the design and the skill of the cutter, one small panel may take as long as four hours to cut out. When cutting out

is finished the glass is ready to be etched. If care has been taken in preparing and cutting out the pattern the result will be worth every minute of the hours of work involved.

This process can be used to provide new door panels, sidelights, fanlights and corner lights for the entrance to a house. The name of the house can be incorporated into the fanlight design in accordance with common practice in the Victorian era. In restoration work care should be taken to ensure that the designs used are appropriate to the period and style of the house. The type of lettering used in etching names into fanlights should also be of an appropriate style. The shapes of letters can be taken from another house or houses and reassembled on cardboard into the original name of the building being restored.

Etched glass is fitted so that the surface which has been treated is on the interior of the building. This minimises the accumulation of dust and grease which could be expected to collect in the shallow depressions created by the action of the acid. For this reason any lettering which is to be etched into glass should be applied to the surface in reverse. It will be seen from the other side and will of course then appear the right way around.

Perhaps the most spectacular effects possible with the etching process were obtained when flashed glass was used. This glass was formed by blowing a bubble of clear glass, then dipping it into molten coloured glass, usually ruby red or blue. The bubble was blown again and expanded before being cut and formed into a sheet. The result was a sheet with clear glass 2–3 mm thick, with a film of coloured glass 0·5 mm or less thick as an integral part of the sheet. Very beautiful effects could be obtained when designs were etched into the thin film of coloured glass.

Etched glass patterns can be preserved by keeping rubbings in a safe place. This will ensure that breakage of the glass does not result in the loss of a precious pattern as it can always be reproduced if a rubbing is available. Photographs also provide useful records.

OTHER DECORATIVE EFFECTS

The use of transfers was well established by the 1880s. These provided a means by which effects similar to those achieved by etching could be obtained without the use of hydrofluoric acid. They were easy to instal or replace in case of breakage.

Transfer papers were printed with designs similar in colour and shape to those obtained by etching flashed glass. They were installed in and around the front door of many houses, sometimes sandwiched between two thin sheets of glass to provide protection against scratching or peeling of the paper. Their durability depended very largely on the life of the glass but where this was preserved or swiftly repaired after cracking or minor damage transfers could last as long as any other form of glass decoration used prior to 1900.

Brilliant cut glass was often seen in the corner lights at a front door. The effect was obtained by using an abrasive wheel or disc to wear away part of the colour on a small square of flashed glass. One of the most common patterns resembled a star. As the pattern was cut into the surface of the glass quite spectacular effects were obtained when brilliant cut designs were illuminated from behind.

Sandblasting offers a possible alternative to etching as a means of decorating glass. Masking tape is the resist used in this case—Bear Brand 250 tape is suitable.

An elaborate Edwardian gas bracket

LIGHTING

The task of ensuring that their homes were satisfactorily lit at night or on gloomy days was a continuing pre-occupation for Australians during the nineteenth century. Houses had to be stocked with supplies of matches, candles, kerosine, lamp oil, wicks, mantles, shades, chimneys and spare lamps. All of this paraphenalia had to be stored in a dry place, easily accessible and ready for use when required. Victorian lighting techniques were inescapably associated with candlegrease, smoke, heat, lack of oxygen and risk of fire. The smoke and heat damaged paint, furniture, furnishings and clothing while the risk of injury from burns or fire was always present.

Disregarding the nuisance and the risks, both of which they were forced to accept, the Victorians had evolved reasonably efficient means of lighting the homes of all but the very poor within their society. The majority of houses in the cities were fitted with gas lighting, supplemented by the use of oil lamps and candles. Argand lamps, fuelled by sperm oil, were largely supplanted by the development of colza, a high quality fuel which was preferred for lighting better-quality rooms in the houses of the upper-middle class.

Typical specifications for a gasfitter, preparing to fit a large house for gaslighting, were described by the architect George Robson in 1876. They have been abridged to deal only with the major living areas but still provide a rare glimpse of the scale and quality of the lighting used in many houses of this era:

Services:—
Ceiling-lights for inner hall and porch outside. To centre of dining-room ceiling with 'Carter's' patent regulating valve, and branches off with 2/8" pipes for bracket-lights to each side of the chimney-breast. ½" supply-pipe for six bracket-lights in drawing-room, as follows:— One on each side of the chimney-breast, one on each angle of bay-window, and two at end of room.

Fittings:—
To the inner hall a Pendant-light of the value of £6. To the porch a Globe-light of the value of £4. To the dining-room a Six-light gaselier, of the value of £10; and for the Bracket-lights to match, each of the value of 30s. To the drawing-room six Bracket-lights, each of the value of £2.[20]

A bracket light was often provided to illuminate the staircase and was usually positioned high up on the opposite wall.

By the 1880s gas had been a fact of life in many houses for forty years. It was widely recognised that gas lighting in bedrooms was dangerous, especially to people in the habit of using a night-light: 'It consumes much oxygen . . . and vitiates the atmosphere . . . . A pair of candles on the mantelpiece, and another pair on the dressing-table, with a box of matches . . . where they can be found in a moment, leave nothing to be desired in the way of convenience.'[21]

Lighting in the drawing room and dining room was far more elaborately contrived. Its importance was emphasised by an English opthalmic surgeon, Robert Carter, who in outlining correct practice in 1883, provides valuable guidance for modern-day restorers of Victorian houses. The importance of lighting the room to suit the occasion was recognised even then:

There is the lighting for the reception of company, as for an evening entertainment, the lighting of a room for a smaller circle, assembled to talk, or to hear music, . . . the lighting of a room for dinner, and the lighting for that daily use in which members of a family may desire to read, to write, or otherwise to apply their eyes to near objects, while others are content to be unemployed.

In lighting up a room for an evening entertainment, as a dance or a *conversazione*, the objects to be secured are that the light should be sufficient to exhibit the beauties of women, of dress, of jewels, and of any pictures or other attractive objects upon the tables or walls; while at the same time it should not occasion distress by being excessive in amount, or by the direction of its rays. . . . the colour of the flame may be controlled at pleasure by the use of coloured globes or chimneys; and in this way many pleasing effects may be produced. My own drawing-room . . . is lighted by ruby lamps, and the roseate tint which they cast over all the objects in the room is extremely pleasing. . . .

The lighting of a dining-room is a matter which should be governed mainly by the style of its decorations . . . . In some dining-rooms, the walls have been regarded merely as affording a frame, or setting, to the central table, which, with its decorations, its linen, its glass and its silver, and its environment of guests, partly consisting of ladies in brilliant toilettes, forms the picture. In others, the walls are adorned by objects upon which it is pleasant to look in the intervals between the courses; and it is manifest that the two styles will require very different treatment . . . .

If the walls are generally decorative, and intended to be looked at during dinner, the best arrangement is to have two or more tall lamps on the sideboard, or on detached columns in other parts of the room, according to its size, together with a central suspended light, not shaded, but left free to throw its illumination upwards and around. In this way, the general lighting of the room and of the wall-surfaces may be accomplished; while that of the table should be secured by a sufficiency of single candles, so placed as not to intercept the view of the guests, and each of which may be covered by a little shade of silk or paper, of crimson or some other warm colour, so as to throw nearly all the light upon the table surface and upon the plates. If there should be any picture of special beauty upon the walls, this should not be left to the general illumination of the upper parts of the room, but should have lights of its own on either side of it—perhaps single gas-burners on brackets projecting from the walls, and furnished with mirrors to illuminate the picture, while they conceal sources of light from the guests. Where the walls are of dark colours, merely adapted to form a frame to the table, it will be sufficient to have two tall lamps on the sideboard; the central light should be shaded, and candles should be placed on the table itself as before.[22]

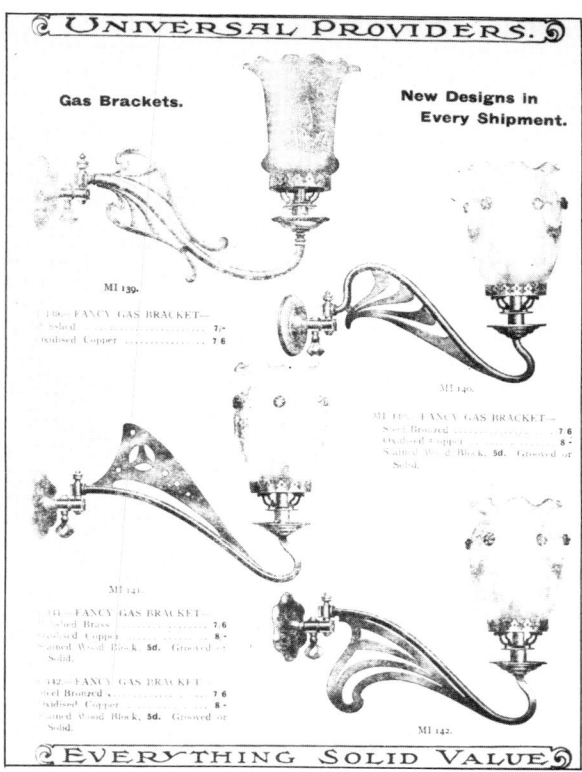

Edwardian gas brackets from the catalogue of F Lassetter and Company of Sydney, 1909

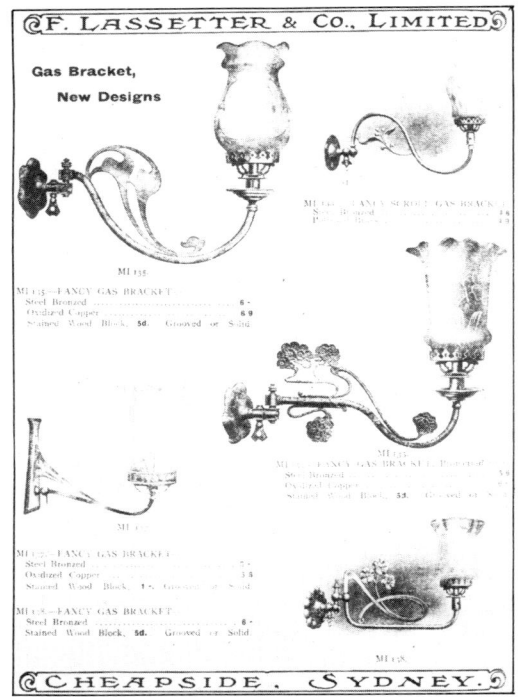
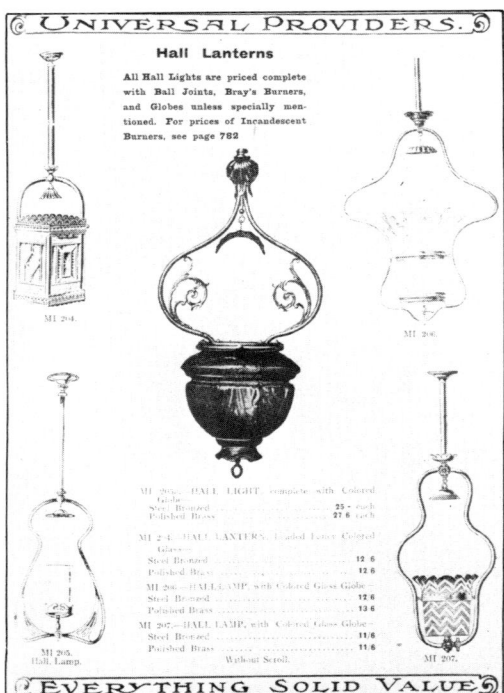
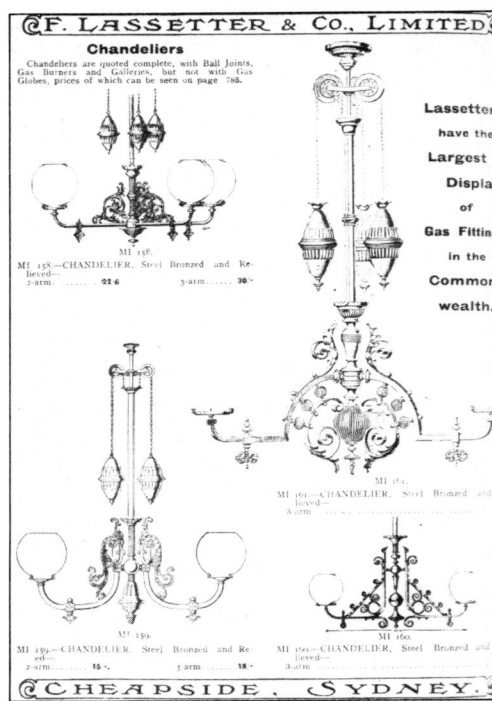

Gas brackets, hall lanterns and gasoliers from the 1909 catalogue of F Lassetter and Company, Sydney. The type and placement of lights was firmly ordered in the Victorian and Edwardian eras

The correct restoration of the hall, drawing room and dining room of a Victorian house, and many Edwardian homes, requires the installation of gas-style lighting. Drawing rooms and dining rooms in all but the largest houses may be fitted with four-branch gasoliers, supplemented if required by bracket lights. The appropriate fittings may be obtained from antique dealers or from a limited number of lighting retailers. Reproduction gasoliers do not have the detail that is the mark of an antique but are less expensive and easier to obtain. Gasoliers may be distinguished from the electroliers of the Edwardian period by the simple fact that their lamps and shades point upwards instead of to the floor. The exception to this rule is the range of gas lights which emulated electroliers. They were described and illustrated in a 1909 catalogue of the Sydney store of F Lassetter and Company: 'Inverted Gas Brackets. The Inverted Incandescent Gas Burner is the latest style of Incandescent Gas Lighting, and has the appearance of Electric Light.'[23]

It is accepted today that gas lighting fittings will have been converted to electricity. It is possible that future trends in restoration, with perhaps a greater emphasis on accuracy in such detail, may result in the increased use of gas lighting in well restored homes. However, the disadvantages of gas lighting are likely to limit any such trend.

As many houses were lit by electricity by 1900, owners of houses dating from this period or later should attempt to determine which form of lighting was originally used in their home. Evidence may take the form of old fittings, wires or pipes which may be hidden under the plaster or out of sight in the ceiling. The records of electricity or gas supply authorities, if accessible, may also be useful.

Many old houses, whether Victorian or Edwardian, have lighting systems which utilise ceiling-mounted switches which are operated by tugging a cord. These may be retained, as, while not necessarily contemporary with the period of the house, they do contribute to the atmosphere of age.

Appendix 1
Some basic advice

The approach to be taken to the practical tasks involved in the restoration of an old house will depend on the personal abilities, interests and finances of the owner. The degree of involvement by architect, builder or skilled tradesmen may largely depend on the funds that are available. As most builders are involved in new construction work they cannot be expected to be familiar with the philosophy of restoration. Careful supervision, preferably by a specialist restoration architect, will probably be necessary.

Because of the uncertainties involved in this type of work, pricing is a very chancy business. Builders quoting for restoration jobs are very likely to think of the highest figure they can justify and then add on a substantial percentage to cover contingencies. If the work goes smoothly they may make a substantial profit. Underquoting can happen—but not very often.

The most economical method of carrying out restoration work is probably a combination of owner involvement and the use of outside tradesmen or contractors. The owner can take personal responsibility for those areas of the work which are time consuming and labour intensive. These may include stripping paint from the staircase, filling holes in render or plaster, minor painting and other tasks which someone with an interest in the building is likely to do better than anyone who is being paid.

It is strongly recommended that tradesmen be employed for carpentry, joinery, bricklaying, stonemasonry, plastering and, of course, plumbing and electrical work. In some cases costs can be minimised if the owner is willing to work with the tradesmen as an unskilled labourer or assistant. Tradesmen may be employed on a day or hourly rate or may give a price for their part of the job. With less scrupulous tradesmen or contractors the latter arrangement can result in hurried and unsatisfactory work. Generally speaking, payment by the day will produce a better job. The disadvantage is that the owner has no prior means of knowing what the total cost will be.

An effective means of obtaining tradesmen is to place advertisements in the positions-vacant columns of the weekend newspapers. Weekend work is often welcomed by tradesmen who are employed by building firms or contractors, particularly if payment is in cash. The advantage of weekend work is that the owner is on hand to answer questions, advise on his or her requirements, obtain needed items from the hardware store or timberyard, and to ensure that the work is properly carried out.

It is advisable to live in a house for a time before work begins in earnest. This helps to identify problems which may not be immediately apparent and will aid in the development of a systematic work programme. One aspect or area of the building should be tackled at a time. Nothing is more depressing than a collection of half-finished jobs. As the New South Wales surveyor G B White said in 1844: 'I do not know anything more calculated to blue devil a man than an unfinished building.'[1] Living in the midst of chaos is unpleasant. The areas of the house that are being worked on should be kept as clean and tidy as possible. Rubble and rubbish can be allowed to accumulate in one area of the yard until there is enough to justify a trip to the tip.

Owners who intend to become involved in the work themselves will find that the following tools and equipment will be useful: hammer, saw, chisels, hacksaw, cold chisel, ladder, tin snips, pliers, nail punches, trowel, paintbrushes and roller, gas burner, set of scrapers, electric drill and an orbital sander. It usually pays to buy quality tools as they last longer and do a better job. A small wheelbarrow may also be worth buying.

The restoration of a dilapidated building which must be occupied throughout the course of the work is not always an enjoyable experience. There will be times when it will seem that the job is never going to be finished. Lack of funds means that private restoration projects may take several years. Photographs taken periodically as a record of work will indicate that excellent progress is being made and that depression is unfounded.

Appendix 2
Directory

The following list contains the names, addresses and telephone numbers of some suppliers of the special products and services which are often needed for the restoration of Victorian and Edwardian houses. It is not an exhaustive list but has been compiled primarily to demonstrate that it is still possible to locate people and companies active in this highly specialised field.

The fact that a service or product is not listed does not necessarily mean that it is not available or is not recommended. The author apologises for any errors or omissions and would welcome suggestions for possible inclusion in any future edition of this directory.

Many of the firms and individuals listed are able to provide a variety of products and services or offer advice on where they may be found. Restoration architects in private practice, or in Government Departments involved in restoration work, will often be able to offer advice and assistance with unusual products, services or tradespeople.

The names of architects who specialise in restoration work may be obtained from offices of the National Trust in state capitals.

ARCHITECTURAL HARDWARE

(See also: Locks)

Antique Brass Company
47 Glebe Point Road
GLEBE, N S W   02 660 1608

Bateman, J and W, Ltd
47 Henry Street
FREMANTLE, W A   09 335 4444

Hanks and Lindsay Pty Ltd
615 Hammond Avenue
WAGGA WAGGA, N S W
069 21 3387

James, J, and Co. Pty Ltd
32 Goulburn Street
SYDNEY, N S W   02 61 6369
403 Pacific Highway
ARTARMON, N S W   02 437 6259
55 Macquarie Street
LEICHHARDT, N S W   02 560 4555

Pearce, F W, Ltd
23 Marlborough Street
ADELAIDE, S A   08 51 6951

Reid, N J, Hardware Pty Ltd
736 Hampton Street
BRIGHTON, VIC.   03 592 6630

Stanco Hardware Co. Pty Ltd
30 Troode Street
WEST PERTH, W A   09 322 6993

BEESWAX

Haymes, Henry, (Victoria) Pty Ltd
57 Rosamond Road
MAIDSTONE, VIC.   03 317 9789

Jacaranda Chemicals Pty Ltd
39 Wellington Street
CHIPPENDALE, N S W   02 69 5094

Wattyl Ltd
4 Steel Street
BLACKTOWN, N S W   02 621 6255

BRASS

POLISHING
Halmark Polishing
137 Regent Street
CHIPPENDALE, N S W   02 698 1007

Kay, Gary
471 High Street
PRAHRAN, VIC.   03 529 4785

Kensey Metalcraft Pty Ltd
1749 Botany Street
BOTANY, N S W   02 666 9613

Metal Finishers (S A) Pty Ltd
19 Ninth Street
BOWDEN, S A   08 46 4075

REPAIR AND FABRICATION
Decorative Brass
Cnr. Quarry Lane and
Henry Avenue
ULTIMO, N S W   02 660 7768

CASTINGS

FERROUS
Cox & Rizzetti Pty Ltd
86 Johnston Street
COLLINGWOOD, VIC.   03 41 3420

Ellery Castings Pty Ltd
55 Drayton Street
BOWDEN, S A   08 46 1361

Glasson's Foundry Pty Ltd
96 Arncliffe Street
ARNCLIFFE, N S W   02 59 4731

Hanks and Lindsay Pty Ltd
615 Hammond Avenue
WAGGA WAGGA, N S W
069 21 3387

Haydon, E, and Co.
59 Robertson Street
KENSINGTON, VIC.   03 376 7459

Lynch, Brian, Foundry Co. Pty Ltd
32 Chifley Drive
PRESTON, VIC.   03 44 7831

McMillan and Co. Foundry
122 Edward Street
BRUNSWICK, VIC.   03 380 4594
Pout, J T, and Co.
18 Gardiner Road
Rutherford, MAITLAND, N S W
049 32 7449
Richmond Ironworks Pty Ltd
3 Paget Street
RICHMOND, N S W   045 78 2640
*Wellington Founders and
Engineering Co. Pty Ltd*
48 Wellington Road
GRANVILLE, N S W   02 632 8863

NON-FERROUS
Adelaide Brass Castings Pty Ltd
100 Gibson Street
BOWDEN, S A   08 46 3846
Adelaide Non-Ferrous Industries
46 Byre Avenue
SOMERTON PARK, S A   08 294 1659
Crystal Star Products Pty Ltd
97 Market Street
SMITHFIELD, N S W   02 604 8716
Delton Industries
160 Musgrave Road
COOPERS PLAINS, QLD.   07 277 2388
Glasson's Foundry Pty Ltd
96 Arncliffe Street
ARNCLIFFE, N S W   02 59 4731
Green, Joseph
8 Atkins Street
RED HILL, QLD.   07 36 5157
Ellery Castings Pty Ltd
55 Drayton Street
BOWDEN, S A   03 46 1361
Jackson's Lock and Brassworks Pty Ltd
106 Cameron Street
LAUNCESTON, TAS.   003 31 7644
Kentcast
196 Victoria Road
MARRICKVILLE, N S W   02 519 4688
Nielsen's Foundry Pty Ltd
58 Gillan Street
NORMAN PARK, QLD.   07 399 5725
Priest, A J, and Co
222 Planet Street
WELSHPOOL, W A   09 361 2439

Reid, N J, Hardware Pty Ltd
736 Hampton Street
BRIGHTON, VIC.   03 592 6630
Swift, J, Diecasters (1975) Pty Ltd
274 Ferntree Gully Road
CLAYTON NORTH, VIC.   03 544 3055
Sydney Lace Reproductions
334 Victoria Road
GLADESVILLE, N S W   02 896 2333

CHIMNEY POTS

Bennett's Magill Pottery Pty Ltd
28 Briant Road
MAGILL, S A   08 31 1340
Mashman, Fred A, Pty Ltd
Mashman Avenue
KINGSGROVE, N S W   02 50 9140

FRENCH POLISH

(*See:* Painting, special effects)

GALVANISED IRON
ROLLED
Byrnes, Harry, Pty Ltd
60a Kent Road
MASCOT, N S W   02 667 4012
Cooper's Tank and Plumbing Works
121 Ryedale Road
WEST RYDE, N S W   02 80 3025
Creek, H W, and Son Pty Ltd
319 Middleborough Road
BOX HILL, VIC.   03 89 0521
Cutler, E H, and Sons
99 Station Road
Silkstone, IPSWICH, QLD.
07 281 3511
Fletcher's Hardware Pty Ltd
50 Oxford Street
EAST SYDNEY, N S W   02 31 9255
Smith and Sons Pty Ltd
135 Newmarket Road
WINDSOR, QLD.   07 57 3148

Stratco
265 West Beach Road
RICHMOND, S A   08 352 4388
Tomlin, J W, Pty Ltd
Loveridge Street
ALEXANDRIA, N S W   02 699 7378
Ward, George, (1964) Pty Ltd
70 Gladstone Street
SOUTH MELBOURNE,
VIC.   03 690 3755
Watkins and Starr Pty Ltd
135 Grange Road
BEVERLEY, S A   08 46 3001

GLASS

DESIGNS FOR ETCHING AND
DECORATING
Evans, Annette
18 Mansfield Street
GLEBE, N S W   02 660 3386

ETCHING AND DECORATING
Adin-James, Chris
323 Clarendon Street
SOUTH MELBOURNE,
VIC.   03 690 2837
Burley, Keith
Glasscrafters Studio
443 Swan Street
RICHMOND, VIC.   03 42 6800
Design Glass
6 Temby Street
BECKENHAM, W A   09 451 2252
Harradence, A E, and Co Pty Ltd
393 Riley Street
SURRY HILLS, N S W   02 211 4572
James, G
81 Montague Road
WEST END, QLD.   07 44 6902
O'Dowd, Bren, and Coffey, Marie
Memory Lane
112 Victoria Road
DRUMMOYNE, N S W   02 81 5570
Thompson and Harvey Ltd
Glass Division
575 Grand Junction Road
GEPPS CROSS, S A   08 381 5222

FLASHED OR LEADLIGHT

Architectural Leadlights Pty Ltd
    Argyle Art Centre
    8 Argyle Street
    SYDNEY, N S W   02 27 4217
Art Glass
    3 Gardiner Avenue
    ST MORRIS, S A   08 332 4186
Bolton Glass Pty Ltd
    549 Liverpool Road
    STRATHFIELD, N S W   02 642 6489
Bromley Simpson and Co. Pty Ltd
    287 Bourke Street
    DARLINGHURST, N S W   02 31 9282
City Glass and Leadlights
    184 Hale Street
    PETRIE TERRACE, QLD.   07 36 2953
Ferguson and Papas
    6 Karma Avenue
    EAST MALVERN, VIC.   03 211 7134
Gowers and Brown
    'Caraboya'
    30 Old York Road
    GREENMOUNT, S A   09 294 1438
Leadlight Studio
    31 Wodonga Avenue
    BEVERLEY, S A   08 45 5416
Leadlights Pty Ltd
    936 Stanley Street
    EAST BRISBANE, QLD.   07 391 4427
Little, Kevin
    Arncliffe Studios
    19 Barden Street
    ARNCLIFFE, N S W   02 599 7348
Stained Glass Shoppe
    311 Fullarton Road
    FULLARTON, S A   08 272 6317
Thompson and Harvey Ltd
    Glass Division
    575 Grand Junction Road
    GEPPS CROSS, S A   08 381 5222
Yencken Sandy Glass Industries Pty Ltd
    637 Gardeners Road
    MASCOT, N S W   02 669 5666

GRAINING
    (*See:* Painting, special effects)

GOLD LEAF

Pierini, Aldo
    9 Hardwicke Street
    BALWYN, VIC.   03 80 2629

GUTTERING, OGEE

Campbell, James, and Sons
    496 Sherwood Road
    SHERWOOD, QLD.   07 37 9888
Creek, E H, and Son Pty Ltd
    319 Middleborough Road
    BOX HILL, VIC.   03 89 0521
Cutler, E H, and Sons
    99 Station Road
    Silkstone, IPSWICH,
        QLD.   07 281 3511
Du Feu Metal
    435 Scarborough Beach Road
    OSBORNE PARK, W A   09 444 4915
Harper, E A, and Sons Pty Ltd
    43 Ashford Avenue
    MILPERRA, N S W.   02 771 3911
Helsby, T, and Son Pty Ltd
    4a Cunningham Street
    SYDNEY, N S W   02 211 1795
Rance, H, and Son Pty Ltd
    478 Hay Street
    SUBIACO, W A   09 381 8055
Stratco
    265 West Beach Road
    RICHMOND, S A   08 352 4388
Ward, George, (1964) Pty Ltd
    70 Gladstone Street
    SOUTH MELBOURNE,
        VIC.   03 690 3755
Watkins and Starr
    135 Grange Road
    BEVERLEY, S A   08 46 3001

JOINERY

ARCHITRAVES, SKIRTINGS,
    MOULDINGS, DOORS, SASHES
    ETC.
Adelaide Joinery Works Pty Ltd
    29 Williams Street
    MILE END, S A   08 352 5555

Allkind Joinery and Glass Pty Ltd
    594 Rode Road
    CHERMSIDE, QLD.   07 59 3025
Australian Joinery Pty Ltd
    17 Sturt Street
    ADELAIDE, S A   08 51 5694
Balmain Joinery Works Pty Ltd
    114 Terry Street
    ROZELLE, N S W   02 82 1279
Bunning Bros Pty Ltd
    Pilbara Street
    WELSHPOOL, W A   09 458 0202
Crescent Timber Co. Pty Ltd
    The Crescent
    ANNANDALE, N S W   02 660 7133
Duce Joinery
    John Street
    BUNDAMBA, QLD.   07 282 1579
Fewings, F J, and Son
    Cnr Victoria and Edmond Streets
    WAVERLEY, N S W   02 389 3393
Gladesville Joinery Pty Ltd
    33 Buffalo Road
    GLADESVILLE, N S W   02 80 4579
Heatherdale Joinery and Builders Supplies
    Molan Street
    RINGWOOD, VIC.   03 870 3644
Kay, Alan, Joinery Pty Ltd
    3 Waratah Street
    WARRIMOO, N S W   047 53 6381
Langdon and Langdon Pty Ltd
    167 New Canterbury Road
    PETERSHAM, N S W   02 560 2444
Lewis, A, and Co. Pty Ltd
    302 Jasper Road
    ORMOND, VIC.   03 578 1155
L B A Joinery Pty Ltd
    11 George Street
    BLACKBURN, VIC.   03 878 0572
*Maribyrnong Timber and
        Building Supplies Pty Ltd*
    58 Emu Road North
    MAIDSTONE, VIC.   03 317 9867
Otto and Co. Pty Ltd
    139 Magill Road
    STEPNEY, S A   08 42 3522
Port Adelaide Joinery Works
    6 Rosetta Street
    ROSEWATER, S A   08 47 2155

Ryde Joinery Works Pty Ltd
12 Dunlop Street
ENFIELD, N S W   02 642 6600
Softwoods Milling Co. Pty Ltd
106 Beattie Street
BALMAIN, N S W   02 82 1234
Walter and Miller
Cnr Darling and Tiger Streets
IPSWICH, QLD.   07 281 3777
W A Wood Mouldings Pty Ltd
634 Hardey Road
KEWDALE, W A   09 458 8522
Whittakers Ltd
271 Treasure Road
WELSHPOOL, W A   09 458 3933

LEAD, SHEET OR STRIP

Lempriere, O T, and Co. Ltd
Offices in capital cities
McIlwraith Industries Pty Ltd
753 Botany Road
ROSEBERRY, N S W   02 699 3111
Stepney Trading Co.
25 Magill Road
STEPNEY, S A   08 42 1277
Thomas Thoms Pty Ltd
83 Morris Street
SUMMER HILL, N S W   02 797 7811
Wool Bay Lime Pty Ltd
1 Blight Street
RIDLEYTON, S A   08 46 0231

LIGHTING

GAS BRACKETS, HALL LIGHTS,
GASOLIERS AND KEROLIERS
Antique Brass Company
47 Glebe Point Road
GLEBE, N S W   02 660 1608
Kay, Gary
471 High Street
PRAHRAN, VIC.   03 529 4785

Portobello Shop of Paddington
94 Hargreave Street
PADDINGTON, N S W   02 32 5462

LOCKS

MAKERS
Harris, A S
72 Fitzroy Street
MARRICKVILLE, N S W   02 51 2379
Jackson's Lock and Brassworks Pty Ltd
106 Cameron Street
LAUNCESTON, TAS.   003 31 7644

REPAIRERS AND KEY CUTTERS
Bridge, R and W, Pty Ltd
128 Parramatta Road
CAMPERDOWN, N S W   02 51 5135
Chantry, Albert, and Co. Pty Ltd
668 Mt Alexander Road
MOONEE PONDS, VIC.   03 370 6033
Jackson's Lock and Brassworks Pty Ltd
106 Cameron Street
LAUNCESTON, TAS.   003 31 7644
Longhurst and Andrew Pty Ltd
159 Broadway
SYDNEY, N S W   02 211 2971
Longshaw, T H, Pty Ltd
455 Pitt Street
SYDNEY, N S W   02 212 3437
Nelson Locksmiths Pty Ltd
333 Halifax Street
ADELAIDE, S A   08 223 5977
Paust and Gibson
15 High Street
FREMANTLE, W A   09 335 1552
Stewart, A F
201 Little Collins Street
MELBOURNE, VIC.   03 63 8771

MANTELPIECES

INSTALLATION OF MARBLE
MANTELPIECES
Wicks, Milton
c/o 64 Australia Avenue
MATRAVILLE, N S W   02 661 2527

MARBLE

(*See also:* Mantelpieces)

CLEANING AND POLISHING
COMPOUNDS
Latham, W, and Co. Pty Ltd
11 Wells Street
ANNANDALE, N S W   02 660 6688

CRAFTSMEN
Bennett, Ron
94 Marlborough Street
SURRY HILLS, N S W   02 698 2115
Hallett, F, and Sons Pty Ltd
25 Bridge Road
RICHMOND, VIC.   03 42 6668
Melocco Bros Pty Ltd
170 Centre Road
SPRINGVALE, VIC.   03 546 0211
Vallario, F, and Co.
47 Jersey Street
HORNSBY, N S W   02 477 1116

MARBLING

(*See:* Painting, special effects)

PAINT

COLOURS MIXED TO ORDER
Crowhurst, W P, Pty Ltd
97 Gouger Street
ADELAIDE, S A   08 51 5255
Dulux Australia Ltd
Sales service offices in
capital cities and
Paint 'n Paper stores
throughout Australia
Pascol Paints
9 Byrne Street
BOTANY, N S W   02 666 8711
Pettigrew, J K, and Sons Pty Ltd
344 Sydney Road
BRUNSWICK, VIC.   03 380 5148

Spartan Paints Pty Ltd
    303 South Road
      MILE END, S A   08 268 6133
Taubmans Ltd
    Decoration and trade centres
    in capital cities and
    some country areas
Universal Paint
    Manufacturing Co. Pty Ltd
    190 Parramatta Road
      CAMPERDOWN, N S W   02 519 5800

SOME TRADITIONAL COLOURS
Walpamur Ltd
    Customer service offices in
    capital cities

FRENCH POLISH, WHITE
Shines Pty Ltd
    14 Cressy Road
      ROSEBERRY, N S W   02 663 2071

SPECIAL FINISHES

BLAC–IT *and* ZEBO
    for grates, stoves and other
    metal objects
O'Brien Manufacturing
    9 Hackett Street
      ULTIMO, N S W   02 660 6108
    (after hours)

BLACK JAPAN
Feast Watson and Co. Pty Ltd
    13–15 Collins Street
      ALEXANDRIA, N S W   02 698 1914
Shines Pty Ltd
    14 Cressy Road
      ROSEBERRY, N S W   02 663 2071

SPECIAL EFFECTS

GRAINING, MARBLING *and*
    STENCILLING
Barrow, Brian
    68a Caledonia Street
      PADDINGTON, N S W   02 326 1053

Crossan, John
    7 Heather Street
    Silkstone, IPSWICH,
      QLD.   07 281 7790
Pettigrew, J K, and Sons Pty Ltd
    372 Sydney Road
      BRUNSWICK, VIC.   03 380 5148
Spindler Pollack and Staff
    1410 Malvern Road
      GLEN IRIS, VIC.   03 20 3378
Stirling-Stevens
    Rear 26 Kippax Street
      SURRY HILLS, N S W   02 211 5351

PAVING
(*See also:* Tiles . . .)

BRICK
Gulson Pty Ltd
    Sydney Road
      GOULBURN, N S W   048 21 3333

PLASTER, DECORATIVE

ROSES, CORNICES, ETC.
Atlas Plaster Co. W A
    Railway Parade
      BAYSWATER, W A   09 279 4422
Ceilings Pty Ltd
    91 Magill Road
      STEPNEY, S A   08 42 3535
Cooper Brothers Pty Ltd
    381 Liverpool Road
      ASHFIELD, N S W   02 798 6191
Derite Pty Ltd
    222 Inglis Street
      PORT MELBOURNE,
        VIC.   03 645 1877
Musgrave Brothers
    38 Love Street
      BULIMBA, QLD.   07 399 4308
Picton Hopkins Australia Pty Ltd
    17 Laity Street
      RICHMOND, VIC.   03 42 3541
    138–46 Bell Street
      PRESTON, VIC.   03 44 5101
    539 Princes Highway

      MORWELL, VIC.   051 34 4318
    Nelson Street
      NUMURKAH, VIC.   058 62 1305
    8 Knoll Street
      GLENORCHY, TAS.   002 72 8100
Plasterers' Supply Co. Pty Ltd
    157 St John's Road
      GLEBE, N S W   02 660 4935
Savage, Chris, Associates
    77 Howe Street
      OSBORNE PARK, W A   09 444 0004
W A Plaster Mills
    120 Claisebrook Road
      EAST PERTH, W A   09 328 5211

PUMPS, SUBMERSIBLE

UNDERFLOOR WATER
Onga (N S W) Pty Ltd
    166 Parramatta Road
      CAMPERDOWN, N S W   02 51 3261

SANDBLASTING, CAST IRON

Cessford Sand Blast and
    Metal Spraying Co
    1 River Street
      RICHMOND, VIC.   03 42 3215
Harradence, A E, and Co. Pty Ltd
    393 Riley Street
      SURRY HILLS, N S W   02 211 4572

SECONDHAND MATERIALS

CAST IRON, JOINERY, MANTELPIECES, ETC.
Jamieson, Reg
    72 Newman Street
      NEWTOWN, N S W   02 519 2628
Regeneration
    177 Clarendon Street
      SOUTH MELBOURNE,
        VIC.   03 699 1019

Resurrection Antiques
103 Dundas Place
ALBERT PARK, VIC.   03 699 9983
Stepney Salvage
Magill Road
NORWOOD, S A   08 42 7399
Whelan the Wrecker
605 Sydney Road
BRUNSWICK, VIC.   03 387 1588
Wolfinger, Steve
Cnr Booth Street and Martin
Avenue
ARNCLIFFE, N S W   02 789 3838
(after hours)

SLATE ROOFING

Edwards, G B
917 High Street
ARMADALE, VIC.   03 20 6884
Green, Roy
54 Grosvenor Street
BALACLAVA, VIC.   03 527 4673
Porter, Maxwell, and Sons
Powers Road
SEVEN HILLS, N S W   02 624 6800
Roofing Slate Co. Pty Ltd
Cnr James and Gipps Street
PYRMONT, N S W   02 660 1716

STONE CONSOLIDANT

ETHYL SILICATE
Dex Australia Pty Ltd
10 Clyde Road
RYDALMERE, N S W   02 638 0548

STUCCO REPAIRS

Mooney, M, and Sons Pty Ltd
168 Gladstone Street
SOUTH MELBOURNE,
VIC.   03 690 2177

TILES, PAVING AND HEARTH

Johnson, H and R, Australia Pty Ltd
35 Lusher Street
CROYDON, VIC.   03 723 4041
contact Mr G J Ellison
Patrick, Alan, Pty Ltd
11 Agnes Street
JOLIMONT, VIC.   03 63 8283

TIMBER

TURNED BALUSTERS, NEWEL POSTS,
HANDRAILS, ETC.
James, David, Pty Ltd
188 Johnston Street
ANNANDALE, N S W   02 660 2549
Mollison, L R, Pty Ltd
44 William Street
HAWTHORN, VIC.   03 818 5440

BENT
*Tasmanian Timber Bending
Works Pty Ltd*
Murray Valley Highway
ECHUCA, VIC.   054 82 3492

VENTILATORS

INTERIOR
Plaster Vent Works
4a Cressy Road
RYDE, N S W   02 80 1378

UNDERFLOOR
*Acme Pest Control and
Builders Pty Ltd*
277 Cleveland Street
REDFERN, N S W   02 698 2905
Bennett's Magill Pottery Pty Ltd
28 Briant Road
MAGILL, S A   08 31 1340

Craig, Harry G
12 Forfar Road
Hamlyn Heights, GEELONG,
VIC.   052 78 2038
Ellery Castings Pty Ltd
55 Drayton Street
BOWDEN, S A   08 46 1361

WALLPAPER

VICTORIAN AND EDWARDIAN
Bond, Arthur E, Pty Ltd
216 Canterbury Road
CANTERBURY, VIC.   03 836 6014
Agent for Cole and Son
(Wallpapers) Pty Ltd, 18
Mortimer Street, London
Wilson's Fabrics and Wallpapers
Showrooms in capital cities
Canberra, Newcastle and
Wollongong.
Agent for Sanderson's of London
and other British
manufacturers

MADE TO ORDER
Masterscreen Pty Ltd
Moor Street
FITZROY, VIC.   03 41 3749

HANGERS
Girling, R J
North Road
LILYDALE, VIC.   03 735 5547
Pettigrew, J K, and Sons Pty Ltd
372 Sydney Road
BRUNSWICK, VIC.   03 380 5148

References

References are given in full the first time they appear. Subsequent references are abbreviated thus: first quotation—'G Lister Sutcliffe, *The principles and practice of modern house construction*, Gresham, London, 1909'; subsequent quotations—'Sutcliffe *House construction*'.

INTRODUCTION

1 J B Barlow, paper presented to the Institute of Architects of N S W, 30 November 1892, in *Australasian Builder and Contractors' News* (*A B C N*) 10 December 1892

AUSTRALIANS IN THEIR HOMES

HOUSING FASHIONS, 1840–1910
1 Charles Eastlake, *Hints on household taste*, Longmans, Green and Co., London, 1868
2 *A B C N*, 10 December 1892
3 Article in *The Australasian*, reprinted in *A B C N*, 28 February 1891
4 Catalogue to exhibition, 'Australian flora in art', Elizabeth Bay House, Sydney, 1977

ARCHITECTS, BUILDERS, HOMEOWNERS, TENANTS AND LANDLORDS
5 *A B C N*, 14 March 1891
6 *A B C N*, 20 August 1892
7 *A B C N*, 26 October 1889
8 *A B C N*, 2 November 1889
9 Denis O'Donovan, lecture, 'Art in building—construction', *Industrial and Technological Museum Lectures*, Samuel Mullen, Melbourne, 1873
10 E S Leyland, F Lightbody, R S Burn, *Working drawings and designs in architecture and building*, Fullarton, Edinburgh and London, 1866
11 James Neild, M D, lecture, 'Dirt and disease', *Industrial and Technological Museum Lectures*, Samuel Mullen, Melbourne, 1873
12 G C Inskip, F R I B A, presidential address, Royal Victorian Institute of Architects, in *A B C N*, 11 July 1891
13 Max Kelly, *A certain Sydney: 1900*, Doak Press, Sydney, 1977
14 James Inglis, *Our Australian cousins*, Macmillan, London, 1880
15 *A B C N*, 30 November 1889
16 Howard Joseland, paper presented to the Sydney Architectural Association, 8 August 1892, in *A B C N*, 13 August 1892

THE PEOPLE AT HOME
17 W S Jevons, Sydney by night: Social survey of Australian cities, 1858, unpublished mss., Mitchell Library, Sydney
18 P G Smith, F R I B A, K D Young, A R I B A, S F Murphy (ed.), *Our homes and how to make them healthy*, Cassell, London, 1883

19 G L Sutcliffe, *The principles and practice of modern house construction*, Gresham, London, 1909

20 Smith, Young, Murphy *Our homes*

21 Sutcliffe *Modern house construction*

22 Smith, Young, Murphy *Our homes*

23 Sutcliffe *Modern house construction*

24 Smith, Young, Murphy *Our homes*

25 Smith, Young, Murphy *Our homes*

THE SURROUNDS

FENCES

1 O'Donovan 'Art in building—construction'

GARDENS

2 Colonel G C Mundy, *Our Antipodes*, Richard Bentley, London, 1852

3 B C Peck, *Recollections of Sydney*, John Mortimer, London, 1850

4 Beatrice Bligh, *Cherish the earth*, Ure Smith, Sydney, 1973

5 O'Donovan 'Art in building—construction'

6 James Nangle, 'City, town and private gardens', *Technical Gazette of N S W*, June and August 1911

7 Nangle 'Gardens'

8 K Fahy, J Birmingham (ed.), *Lithgow pottery: Three early catalogues from New South Wales*, Australian Society for Historical Archaeology, Sydney, 1974

9 Fahy, Birmingham *Lithgow pottery*

STRUCTURE

MASONRY

1 O'Donovan 'Art in building—construction'

TIMBER

2 E W Rudder, letter to Colonial Secretary, 14 February 1838, N S W Archives 4/2393

3 Major Henry Oakes, Crown Lands Commissioner, letter to Colonial Secretary, 21 September 1838, N S W Archives 4/2393

4 Mundy *Our Antipodes*

5 'Some ornamental timbers of N S W', *A B C N*, 8 August 1891

6 James Nangle, *Australian building practice*, George Robertson and Co., Melbourne, 1900

FINISHES

ROOFING

1 *A B C N*, 10 December 1892

2 *Zions' Building Trades Pocket Directory*, Louis Zions, Sydney, 1908–09

3 J B Barlow, paper presented to Institute of Architects, N S W, 30 November 1892, in *A B C N*, 10 December 1892

4   *Zions' N S W Building Trades Pocket Directory and Note Book*, Louis Zions, Sydney, 1905–06

5   James Nangle, 'Roof coverings', *Proceedings*, Engineering Association of N S W, vol 10, Sydney 1894–95

6   Robert Irving, 'Early galvanized iron in Australia', *Newsletter*, Royal Australian Historical Society, Sydney, April 1978

WALLS: STUCCO AND PLASTER

7   James Nangle, 'The ornamental treatment of bricks', *Proceedings*, Engineering Association of N S W, vol. viii, Sydney, 1893

8   J Horbury Hunt, Newspaper cuttings, 1860–94, Mitchell Library

9   Nangle 'Bricks'

JOINERY

10   R Riddell, *The carpenter and joiner, stair builder and handrailer*, Thomas C. Jack, Edinburgh, 1870

11   W B Tuthill, *The suburban cottage, its design and construction*, William Comstock, New York, 1885

FIREPLACES

12   O'Donovan   'Art in building—construction'

13   N Arnott, *On the smokeless fireplace*, Longman, Brown, Green and Longmans, London, 1855

14   *A B C N*, 24 December 1892

15   T A Sisley, 'The Australian home', *Building, Engineering and Mining Journal*, 20 December 1890

16   Charles Mayes (compiler), *Australasian Builders' and Contractors' Price Book*, George Robertson, Melbourne, 1891

17   *A B C N*, 23 January 1892

18   Catalogue and price list, Saxton and Binns Ltd, Sydney, 1905

19   Count Rumford, *Of chimney fireplaces, and the principles of chimney construction* (1796), quoted by Valentine Fletcher, *Chimney pots and stacks*, Centaur Press, Fontwell, Sussex, 1968

20   E Dobson, A Hammond, F Walker, *The practical brick and tile book*, Crosby Lockwood and Co., London, 1886

HARDWARE

21   Eastlake   *Household taste*

22   *An encyclopaedia of locks and builders' hardware*, Josiah Parkes and Sons Ltd, Willenhall, England, 1968

23   *A B C N*, 2 July 1892

24   *A B C N*, 7 May 1892

25   Mundy   *Our Antipodes*

26   James Nangle, 'Some notes on healthy house building', *Medical Journal of Australia*, 31 March 1917

27   George Robson, *Modern domestic building construction*, Batsford, London, 1876

28   Colonel H C Seddon, *Builders' work and the building trades*, Rivingtons, London, 1889

DECORATION

PAINTING

1 Harold Atkinson, 'Painting as applied to external decoration', *The decorator's assistant*, London, circa 1880

2 James W Facey, *Practical house decoration*, 4th ed., Crosby Lockwood and Son, London, 1906

3 W L Savage, *Graining and marbling: A complete and practical guide*, Austin Rogers and Co., London, 1925

4 Savage *Graining*

5 James W Facey, *Practical house painting: A guide to the art of ornamental painting*, Crosby Lockwood and Son, London, 1906

TILES

6 Nangle *Australian building practice*

7 *Sands' Sydney Directory*, 1867

8 *A B C N*, 28 December 1889

9 *A B C N*, 7 January 1888

10 *Zions' Building Trades Pocket Directory*, 1908–09

CAST IRON

11 Denis O'Donovan, lecture, 'Art in building—ornamentation', *Industrial and Technological Museum Lectures*, Samuel Mullen, Melbourne, 1873

12 Sisley 'Australian home'

13 Nangle, in *A B C N*, 20 May 1893

14 Nangle *Australian building practice*

15 H C Kent, lecture, in *Architecture*, journal of the Institute of Architects of N S W, November 1924

GLASS

16 'Glass painting as a means of decoration', *A B C N*, 9 June 1888

17 'Glass painting', *A B C N*

18 'Glass painting', *A B C N*

19 James Callingham, *Sign writing and glass embossing*, Simpkin, Marshall and Co., London, 1871

LIGHTING

20 Robson *Modern domestic building construction*

21 Robert Brudenell Carter, S F Murphy (ed.), *Our homes and how to make them healthy*, Cassell, London, 1883

22 Carter, Murphy *Our homes*

23 *Lassetter's Monthly Commercial Review*, no. 4, F Lassetter and Co., Sydney, 1909

APPENDIX 1: SOME BASIC ADVICE

1 G B White, journal, 22 September 1844, Mitchell Library

Sources of Illustrations

The following people, libraries and commercial organisations provided illustrations and gave their consent for reproduction. Historic photographs, in most cases, came from the relevant State Library or specialist historical library such as the Battye Library, Perth, Latrobe Library, Melbourne, Mitchell Library, Sydney, or the John Oxley Library, Brisbane. Illustrations from old journals and catalogues, such as the Australasian Builder and Contractors' News and Lasseter's Monthly Commercial Review, were provided by the Mitchell Library. The photograph of Pembroke Terrace on p 14 and the cedar tree on p 50 were made available by the NSW Government Printer. The majority of new photographs of Sydney buildings and details were taken by Patrick Crowe; those taken in Melbourne are by Pat McArdell.

Australian House and Garden magazine 99.

Battye Library, Perth 36, 61, 83, 107.

Patrick Crowe 11, 12, 13, 15, 16, 17, 20, 29, 32, 34, 36 (2), 37 (2), 38 (2), 40, 41, 45, 46, 47, 57 (2), 58, 59, 60, 62, 63, 64, 67, 69, 71, 72, 73, 75, 76 (2), 77, 78, 79, 80, 82, 86 (2), 87, 89, 90, 91, 92 (2), 93, 95, 97, 104, 106 (3), 107 (2), 109, 110, 111, 112, 114, 115, 116, 117 (2), 119, 120, 121, 122.

Pat McArdell 35, 37, 38, 39 (2), 40, 42, 44 (2), 48, 64, 66, 67, 70, 87, 94, 113 (2), 116.

NSW Government Printer 14, 50.

Hamilton — Smith and Associates 118.

Latrobe Library, Melbourne 2 — 3, 19, 20 (2), 65.

Mitchell Library, Sydney 1, 5, 6, 8, 9, 10, 14, 15, 17 (2), 18 (2), 19 (2), 21, 22, 24 — 25, 26, 27 (2), 32, 35, 36, 40, 41, 42, 43, 49, 50, 51 (2), 53, 55, 56, 68 (3), 72, 74, 81, 82 (3), 83 (3), 84, 85, 89, 91 (2), 92, 93 (2), 94, 95, 96, 97, 99, 100, 102, 105, 108, 111, 116, 123, 124 (3), 125.

National Trust of Australia (NSW) (Photos by J. Whitelock unless stated otherwise) 16, 43, 45, 52, 53, 68, 73, 80 (Douglas Baglin), 81 (Douglas Baglin), 96, 114, 115, 121 (2).

John Oxley Library, Brisbane 23 (2), 24 (2), 25 (2), 33, 51.

Pascol Paints 98, 112.

State Library of NSW 43, 66, 69, 75, 108, 111.

State Library of South Australia 16, 23, 25, 29, 54, 56, 106.

Alan Townsend 30 (2), 70, 88.

State Library of Tasmania 21, 23 (2), 26, 26 — 27, 28, 31 (2), 33, 39, 41, 46, 47, 85, 103.

Neville Waller 100, 100 — 101, 101.

Select bibliography

BIBLIOGRAPHIES

SAUNDERS, D Architectural History; Domestic Architecture Sydney, Author, 1969

CATALOGUES

Beautiful homes Wunderlich Patent Ceiling and Roofing Company; Sydney; 1906

Catalogue of decorative plaster products Picton Hopkins Pty Ltd; Melbourne; 1978

Catalogue of reproduction castings Hanks and Lindsay Pty Ltd; Wagga Wagga, N S W; 1978

Fifty modern ideal cottage homes Kauri Timber Company Ltd; Sydney; 1901

Illustrated catalogue of chimney pots and air bricks Fred A Mashman Pty Ltd; Kingsgrove, N S W; circa 1960

Lassetter's monthly commercial review F Lassetter and Co.; Sydney; 1906, 1909, 1911, 1913, 1914 [Catalogue of a large retail establishment.]

Prices 1905 Saxton and Binns Ltd; Pyrmont, N S W [Timber, joinery and builders' supply merchants.]

DIRECTORIES

Victorian Contractors' and Builders' Price Book C T Mayes; Collingwood, Victoria; 1859, 1862, 1877, 1883, 1886, 1891, 1908 [Also known as the *Australian Builders' and Contractors' Price Book.*]

Zions' Building Trades Pocket Directory, 1908–09 Louis Zions; Sydney

MISCELLANEOUS

IMASHEV, G, *and* SCULTHORPE, G *New South Wales Museum's Resource Directory* Macleay Museum, University of Sydney; Sydney; 1977

Lead roofing The Lead Development Association; London; 1972

PERIODICALS

Australasian Builder and Contractors' News, 1887–95
Building, Engineering and Mining Journal, 1888–1905

BOOKS

CARPENTRY AND JOINERY

MOWATT, W and A *A treatise on stairbuilding and handrailing* George Bell; London; 1900

NEWLANDS, J *The carpenter and joiner's assistant* Blackie and Son; London; 1880

RIDDELL, R *The carpenter and joiner, stair builder and handrailer* Thomas Jack; Edinburgh; 1870

CAST IRON

OWEN, MICHAEL *Antique cast iron* Blandford Press; Poole, Dorset; 1977

ROBERTSON, E GRAEME, *and* JOAN *Cast iron decoration: A world survey* Thames and Hudson; Melbourne; 1977

CERAMICS AND ARCHITECTURAL POTTERY

BOURRY, E *Treatise on the ceramic industries* Scott, Greenwood and Co.; London; 1901

FLETCHER, VALENTINE *Chimney pots and stacks* Centaur Press; Fontwell, Sussex; 1968

Leadless decorative tiles, faience and mosaic W J Furnivall; Stone, Staffordshire; 1904

LEFEVRE, L *Architectural pottery* Scott, Greenwood and Co.; London; 1900

SEARLE, A B *An encyclopaedia of the ceramic industries*, vols 1–3 Ernest Benn Limited; London; 1929–30

Visit to the Fowler Potteries, Marrickville, A R Fowler Ltd; Sydney; circa 1935

CHIMNEYS AND FIREPLACES

ARNOTT, N *On the smokeless fireplace* Longman, Brown, Green and Longmans; London; 1855

CHRISTIE, W W *Chimney design and theory* D Van Nostrand, New York/E and F N Spon, London; 1899

FLETCHER, VALENTINE *Chimney pots and stacks* Centaur Press; Fontwell, Sussex; 1968

PUTNAM, J P *The open fireplace* James Osgood; Boston; 1881

RISING DAMP

HEIMAN, J, WATERS, E and MCTAGGART, R 'The treatment of rising damp', *Architectural Science Review*, vol 16 Research Publications; Melbourne; December, 1973

Information about masonry treatments Dow Corning Australia Pty Ltd; Sydney; 1975
Technical bulletin.

MCTAGGART, R and ARMSTRONG, L 'Rising Damp', *Rebuild*, vol 1, no 5 Division of Building Research, C S I R O; Highett, Vic.; October, 1976

Maintaining and restoring masonry walls National Trust of Australia (N S W); Sydney; 1978

Silicone impregnation to cure rising damp Dow Corning Australia Pty Ltd; Sydney; circa 1970

GENERAL CONSTRUCTION AND BACKGROUND TEXTS

ADDY, S O *Evolution of the English house* E P Publishing Ltd; London; 1975

AUDSLEY, W J and G A *Cottage, lodge and villa architecture* William Mackenzie; London; 1870

BURN, R S *Colonists' and emigrants' handbook of the mechanical arts* William Blackwood and Sons; Edinburgh; 1854

EYLAND, E S, LIGHTBODY, F and BURN, R S *Working drawings and designs in architecture* A Fullarton; Edinburgh; 1866

HADDON, ROBERT *Australian architecture* George Robertson and Co.; Melbourne; 1905

HERMAN, MORTON *The Blackets: An era of Australian architecture* Angus and Robertson; Sydney; 1963

KIDDER, F *Building construction and superintendence* William T Comstock; New York; 1896

MURPHY, SHIRLEY (ed.) *Our homes and how to make them healthy* Cassell; London; 1883

NANGLE, JAMES *Australian building practice* G Robertson; Melbourne; 1900.
[Subsequently various editions published by William Brooks and Co through to 1946.]

PREVOST, R A *Australian bungalow and cottage home designs* The N S W Bookstall Co. Ltd; 1912

ROBSON, G *Modern domestic building construction* Batsford; London; 1876

SEDDON, H *Builders' work and the building trades*, vols 1–8 Rivingtons; London; 1889

SUTCLIFFE, G LISTER *Principles and practice of modern house construction* Gresham Publishing; London; 1909

TUTHILL, W *The suburban cottage, its design and construction* William T Comstock; New York; 1885

GLASS

CALLINGHAM, J *Sign writing and glass embossing* Simpkin, Marshall and Co.; London; 1871

GICK, JAMES E *Creating with stained glass* Gick Publishing Inc.; Laguna Hills, California; 1976

MCGRATH, R and FROST, C *Glass in architecture and decoration* Architectural Press; London; 1937

LOCKS AND KEYS

CHUBB, JOHN *On the construction of locks and keys* W Clowes and Sons; London; 1850

Encyclopaedia of locks and builders' hardware Josiah Parkes and Sons Ltd; Willenhall, England; 1958

TOWNE, H R *Locks and builders' hardware* John Wiley and Sons; New York; 1904

PAINTING

EATON, C H *Painting and decorating*, vols 1 & 2 Pitman; London; 1929

GEESON, A *Practical painter and decorator* Virtue; London; 1937

HOBBS, E W *Practical graining and marbling* Foulsham; London; 1953

HURST, G H *Painters' colours, oils and varnishes* Griffin; London; 1892

JENNINGS, A S *Paint and colour mixing* Spon; London; 1921

PETRIE, J *Practical arts of graining and marbling* Trade Papers Publishing Co. Ltd; London; 1905

SAVAGE, W L *Graining and marbling* Austin Rogers and Co.; London; 1925

SMITH, J C *The manufacture of paint* Scott, Greenwood and Co.; London; 1901

TERRY, G *Pigments, paint and painting* Spon; London; 1893

PLASTER

BURN, R S *The new guide to masonry, bricklaying and plastering* John G Murdoch; London; 1868–72

VERRALL, W *The modern plasterer* Caxton; London; circa 1930

VERRALL, W *Plastering* (reprinted from *Brickwork, concrete and masonry*) Pitman; London; circa 1920

RESTORATION

BRAUN, HUGH S *The restoration of old houses* Faber and Faber Limited; London; 1954

BULLOCK, O M *The restoration manual* Silvermine Publishers; Norwalk, Connecticut; 1966

INSALL, D W *The care of old buildings* Architects' Journal, for the Society for the Protection of Ancient Buildings; London; 1958

LUCAS, CLIVE *Conservation and restoration of buildings* Australian Council of National Trusts; Sydney; 1978

Maintaining and restoring masonry walls National Trust of Australia (N S W); Sydney; 1978

Notes on the preservation and maintenance of old buildings National Trust of Australia (N S W); Sydney; 1965

Renovating a Federation style house National Trust of Australia (N S W); Sydney; 1978

TANNER, HOWARD *and* COX, PHILLIP *Restoring old Australian houses and buildings: An architectural guide* Macmillan; Melbourne; 1975

TECHNICAL PUBLICATIONS

The Commonwealth Experimental Building Station produces an excellent series of technical pamphlets in the series 'Notes on the science of building'. These are available from the Experimental Building Station, P O box 30, Chatswood, N S W, 2067; from Australian Government Publishing Service bookshops in capital cities; by mail from Mail Order Sales, Australian Government Publishing Service, P O box 84, Canberra, A C T, 2600. The following E B S pamphlets contain much helpful advice:

N S B No. 11 *White ants*
N S B No. 26 *Wood borers*
N S B No. 31 *Domestic fireplaces and chimneys*
N S B No. 39 *Damp-proof courses and flashings*
N S B No. 45 *Timber floors in dwellings*
N S B No. 52 *Dampness in buildings*
N S B No. 59 *Cleaning of brickwork*
N S B No. 71 *Plaster mixes*
N S B No. 147 *Paints*
N S B No. 148 *Paint systems: A guide to good practice*

The Forestry Commission of New South Wales, 93 Clarence Street, Sydney, has a range of technical publications which can be useful in coping with some of the problems encountered in restoration work. The following are of particular interest.

No. 3 *Finishes for wooden floors*
No. 10 *Flooring timbers of New South Wales*
No. 11 *Ventilation under timber floors*
No. 12 *The maintenance of wood floors*

No. 14 *Subterranean termites and their control in New South Wales*

No. 15 *Prevention of termite attack in houses and other buildings*

No. 18 *Timber borers of common occurrence*

The Standards Association of Australia produces publications which set out established standards for many aspects of building work. These range from the sanding of wooden floors and the plastering of walls to the standard for paint discussed in the chapter on painting. Details of these and other publications are available from offices of the Association in each of the State capital cities.

Glossary

architrave Decorative timber moulding surrounding a window or doorway.

art nouveau A decorative style, the forms of which are characterized by the use of undulating shapes similar to those seen in waves, flames, or the stalks of plants.

ashlar Stone which has been wrought to square corners and even faces, and laid in horizontal courses with fine mortar joints.

ash pan A flat metal tray with upright sides used to catch ash from fires in a nineteenth-century cast-iron grate.

attic A room within the roof of a building.

awning (see also: *verandah*) A roof with an open side, supported by posts, brackets or cantilevering.

baluster One of the vertical supports, usually of timber or iron, between the newel posts of a staircase and which carry the handrail. Also used to refer to the pear or urn-shaped pillars of stone or concrete which support a railing.

balustrade A series of balusters supporting a handrail or coping.

barge-board A protective piece of timber, often decorated with fretwork, placed against the incline of the gable of a roof and concealing the horizontal roof timbers.

bay An angular or curved projection of a house-front, containing windows. When on an upper story only, called an oriel.

bearers The heavy timbers supporting floor joists.

bond The method of overlapping bricks or stone to tie them together in a wall.

bullnose, -d 1. Used to describe corrugated galvanised-iron which has been curved through ninety degrees for use on the roof of a verandah or balcony. 2. A brick with a rounded corner; used for rounded corners on the exterior of a building.

bungalow From the Hindustani *bangla*, 'belonging to Bengal'—a Bengal house. Derived from the light dwellings with verandahs erected for the British administrators in India.

bridge-ward Adjective used to describe a type of key commonly used in the nineteenth century. Each key was incised in a pattern which corresponded with the mechanism or wards of a lock.

cames Strips of lead used as the structural support in leadlight or stained glass work.

capital The head or crowning feature of a column. Often seen beneath the decorative cast iron friezes at the front of a house, or the timber ornamentation of Federation-style houses.

casement A window hinged on one of its edges so as to open either inwards or outwards.

cast iron Iron formed into a shape by pouring it when molten into a mould. Decorative cast iron is often mistakenly described as wrought iron.

chimneypiece (see: *mantelpiece*)

colonnade A series of columns and their superstructure.

coping A cap or covering to a wall, either flat or sloping to shed water.

cornice A projecting decorative feature joining the top of a wall to the ceiling.

cowl A metal object occasionally used in place of a chimney pot on top of a chimney.

dado The lower part of an internal wall which has been finished or decorated up to about waist height in a manner different to the rest of the wall.

dampcourse A protective barrier in a wall, designed to prevent moisture rising from the ground into the wall.

dressing The smoothing and finishing of stone which is to be used as an element in the decoration of walls, around arches, or in the frames for doors and windows.

eaves The projecting edges of a roof which hang over the walls.

electrolier (see also: *gasolier*) The central light of a room, usually with a brass frame, suspended from the ceiling, and on which there were two or more bulbs. The term was introduced shortly after the availability of electric power for home lighting. It derives from the *gasolier* or kerolier which it replaced.

embossed glass (see: *etched glass*)

encaustic The process by which decorative tiles or bricks are produced by firing them in a kiln.

escutcheon A keyhole plate, often shaped like a shield.

etched glass Glass on which decorative patterns have been produced by the action of hydrofluoric acid.

fanlight In Georgian architecture, a fan-shaped window or 'light' over the front door. Now used to apply to a rectangular window above any door.

fascia A flat piece of timber used on edge to finish the edge of a roof, and to which the guttering is usually attached.

Federation An Australian style of architecture popular in the period between 1890 and 1910. Its features include the use of terracotta tiles, rich red brickwork, and fretted and turned decorative timber.

finial The ornament at the apex of a roof, pediment or gable.

flashed 1. Clear glass with a thin film of coloured glass on one surface. 2. The process by which part of a roof, balcony, etc, has been waterproofed by the use of lead or other form of *flashing*.

flashing Strips of lead, aluminium or other substance used to prevent water access between horizontal and vertical elements on a roof as, for example, around a chimney.

flue The square or rectangular passage in a chimney through which hot air, smoke and gases escape.

footings In effect, the feet of a building; its foundations, usually consisting of a wider course of stone, brick or concrete at the base of a wall.

fretwork Decorative elements, usually of timber, from which portion has been cut away to form a regular pattern. Often used on Federation style houses.

frieze 1. A band of decoration, painted, sculptured or of paper, used on internal walls above the dado or below the cornice. 2. The middle division of a Classical entablature, often decorated. 3. The skirt of cast-iron decoration often depending from the roof of a verandah or balcony.

gable The triangular portion of a wall at the end of a pitched roof.

galvanise Technically, the coating of metal by electro-chemical action. In practice, so-called galvanised iron is produced by coating iron with zinc, by dipping or spraying.

gas bracket A small gas light with one burner and which is fixed to the wall.

gasolier (see also: *electrolier*) The central light of a room, usually with a brass frame, suspended from the ceiling, and holding two or more gas burners.

Georgian Architecture, furniture, silver or decoration dating from the reign of the first three Hanoverian Kings of England (1714–1820), or of architecture of a later date in the style of that period.

Gothic Revival An eighteenth- and nineteenth-century revival of the mediaeval movement in architecture and art.

graining A method of painting by which inexpensive timber was provided with the grain and appearance of a higher quality species. Thus, pine could be 'grained' to resemble mahogany or other quality timbers.

japan A type of paint or varnish used to provide a hard black glossy finish.

joiner A craftsman in timber who does lighter and more ornamental work than a carpenter.

joinery The interior timber fittings and fixtures of a house which have been made and installed by a joiner. Also, a business enterprise conducted by a joiner.

joists The horizontal timbers, laid on edge, on which are nailed the floorboards, or to the underneath of which a ceiling may be fixed.

keystone The middle stone in an arch.

label mould A projecting moulding on the face of an external wall, above a window, arch or doorway. A decorative feature with the functional task of carrying rainwater off the wall. Also known as hood mould.

leadlight A window or 'light' consisting of small coloured pieces of glass held together in a decorative pattern by lead strips or 'cames'.

light The glazed area of a window through which light is admitted to a building.

lintel The horizontal member that spans an opening.

mantelpiece The ornamental structure of marble, timber, cast iron or plaster which extends over and around a fireplace.

masonry Building work in brick or stone.

marbling The process by which timber is painted to resemble marble of various types.

moulding Decorative shapes in plaster or timber which are used to add interest to a wall or other surface. Each style and period of architecture produces characteristic mouldings.

newelpost The principal post at the end of a flight of stairs. It supports the handrails and the outer string upon which the steps rest. Also, the central pillar from which the steps of a winding, or spiral, stair radiate.

ogee A double-curved moulding, concave above and convex below. It provided a very popular pattern for guttering in the nineteenth century.

oriel A bay window on an upper story.

palisade A fence of vertical, pointed wooden stakes or metal rods. A very common form of domestic fencing in nineteenth-century Australia, particularly in urban areas.

parapet A low wall erected to protect or complete any edge where there is a sudden drop, as on a roof.

party wall The common dividing wall between attached houses.

pointing Strong mortar finishing given to the exterior of joints in brickwork.

portico A porch supported by columns and open on at least one side.

purlins Used in roofing to denote the transverse horizontal timbers upon which the battens for the slates, tiles, iron or other covering are fastened.

Regency   The elegant architectural style which evolved when George IV was Prince Regent (1811–20). Also used for the period of his reign.

render   1. The coat of mortar or stucco applied to protect an external wall, often of soft, porous sandstock brick, from the effects of the elements. Usually lined or marked to simulate stone blocks. 2. The first coat of plaster on an internal wall.

resist   The coating applied to the surface of glass which is to be etched by the action of hydrofluoric acid.

ridge   The line at which two intersecting planes of a roof meet.

riser (see also: *tread*)   The vertical or rising part of a step, filling in the gap between the treads.

rose, ceiling   The plaster or metal fixture of various shapes, sizes and patterns used to decorate the centre of a ceiling and from which the main light of a room is suspended.

sarking   A supplementary protective waterproof membrane beneath the main roof material.

sash   The frame which holds the glass of a window, especially in the case of a frame which moves vertically. Hence *sash window*, a window consisting of two or more vertically-sliding sashes.

shingles   Thin pieces of wood with parallel sides used for roofing.

shutter   A louvred frame of wood hinged to swing in front of windows and doors, to provide protection and privacy, or to exclude light.

sill   The lower horizontal part of a window opening.

skirting   Flat board placed against the wall at the point where it meets the floor. Usually moulded at the top.

staple   That part of a lock system which is attached to the frame of a door, and in which the tongue of the lock engages.

string   A sloping structural member at each end of the treads and risers of a staircase.

stucco   A coarse plaster or render composed of a mix of gypsum, lime and cement used to cover the external surfaces of walls. Usually lined to simulate the appearance of stone blocks.

terrace   A row of houses with party walls and with an appearance of architectural uniformity.

tesselated tiles   Tiles of different shapes and colours laid on a path, verandah or floor to form a mosaic pattern. Also called *tesserae*.

tread (see also: *riser*)   The flat, horizontal part of stairs or steps on which the feet are placed.

turned   Wood which has been shaped while revolving in a lathe.

turret   A small tower, usually round or in the shape of a polygon.

valance   A pendant border, fringe or edging. When applied to cast iron, refers to that part of the decorative ironwork which is attached to the underside of a verandah or balcony roof beam.

verandah   An external awning attached to a wall of a building on one side and supported on its outer edge by posts.

vernacular   The unsophisticated architecture of the country.

villa   Originally the farmhouse on an Italian country estate. In nineteenth-century Australia the term implied a detached house or larger cottage, standing in its own ground in a suburban environment.

weatherboard   Overlapping boards, usually horizontal, covering the exterior of a timber-framed wall.

wrought-iron   Iron formed into shape by the use of hand tools and heat. Often mistakenly used to describe cast-iron decoration.

Index